Dear Friends And Family

The Journal Of
ELCA Global Mission Volunteer
Jerry L. Schmalenberger

Jerry L. Schmalenberger

CSS Publishing Company, Inc., Lima, Ohio

DEAR FRIENDS AND FAMILY

For more information about CSS Publishing Company resources, visit our website at www.csspub.com.

ISBN 0-7880-1811-6

PRINTED IN U.S.A.

This collection is dedicated to the memory of the following courageous mission-minded pioneers of the eighteenth and nineteenth centuries:

Morris Officer, Liberia, West Africa

Anna Kugler, India

Ludwig Ingwer Nommensen, Apostle to the Bataks, Sumatra

John Matthias Armbruster, Argentina

Minnie E. Tack, China

Herman Hammer, Uruguay

Justinian Ernst von Weltz, Suriname

Marjorie Bly, Taiwan

Conrad Wilhelm Löehe, Franconia, Germany

Karl L. Reichelt, Tau Fong Shan, New Territories, Hong Kong

Anna Martinson, China and Hong Kong

Table Of Contents

Introduction

"Dear Friends and Family,"

That's the way I began the many faxes and e-mails which I sent to my wife, kids, grandkids and close friends in order to keep contact while I was separated from them. With the present technology to forward messages easily, these reports were dispatched on to an ever-increasing audience. And the prodigious response to them was amazing.

It all began with my retirement from the presidency of Pacific Lutheran Theological Seminary in 1996. I now had the time and interest to volunteer for overseas teaching. The many PLTS contacts with international students and faculties during my sabbaticals brought numerous invitations.

The Evangelical Lutheran Church in America's "Global Mission Volunteer" program gave me the credibility and backing to pursue my interest in teaching and preaching across cultures and languages. A passion for discipling ministry further motivated this preacher of 41 years.

I have tried to report as honestly as possible my experiences and also to write close to the ground and from the heart. I wanted my family not only to picture the experiences but also feel the ambience. I hope it is reporting which is alert to the sensibilities of my precious sisters and brothers overseas. That is a very difficult task for us often arrogant Americans.

So here is a celebration of our oneness in the Christ, in the human global family of many religions, and of a love and delight in being a member of such a rich world wide community.

Very special thanks to my wife Carol, who not only saw the possibility of sharing these stories with a wider audience but also edited them for improved felicity of language and clearness of thought. She often encouraged me to go and gave strong support from our home in California.

As disciples we are directed to "Go and make disciples of all nations ..." (Matthew 28:19). In doing so we may be a blessing to others but I'm sure the greater blessing is to us who go.

— Jerry Schmalenberger

Letters from Indonesia

July 14, 1997
Dear Friends and Family,

I am here at the HKBP (Huria Kristen Batak Protestan) Seminary experiencing yet another new culture. I left at 1:30 a.m. Monday July 7, and the trip over was grueling — fifteen flying hours to Hong Kong, four more to Singapore, an all day wait mostly in the airport with a free tour of the city, and then a one hour flight to Medan, Sumatra. The vice principal who met me drove for three hours to the school at Pematang Siantar, arriving at 11:00 p.m. their time Tuesday evening. School started on Thursday and I taught Friday and Saturday.

Classroom and Library at STT-HKBP Seminary

The principal of the seminary is Robinson Radjagukguk who had PLTS colleague Bob Smith as an advisor at Concordia, St. Louis, and then finished his education (Th.D.) at Chicago.

9

One hundred eighty graduates took the exam to enter this school and sixty were approved. They were divided into three groups, so I have three classes a day each lasting two hours. I teach English six days a week. For the students, the day's schedule begins at 5:45 a.m. with exercise and continues until 21:50 (9:50 p.m.) with spiritual guidance. There will be nineteen faculty here after this preparation for new students portion is completed. While it is a rigorous teaching schedule, the nights are long and rather lonely. The school is much like the Theological College of the West Indies or Gbarnga in Liberia. One-fourth are women. The country's culture is very Muslim and I wake each day to the 4:30 a.m. call to prayer coming from the town's loud speaker.

Like all third world (and some first world) seminaries, everything leaks, is moldy, and most machinery no longer functions. But there is singing and preaching of the Word and a deep piety I so admire in these beautiful people. They are gentle and smart.

I get the Voice of America once a day on my short wave radio and keep up with the news.

My asthma doesn't seem any worse or better than in any other location or climate.

I attended an Indonesian language service today early morning and then a Batak one later. I am so surprised how easily I can sing their hymns in their language from their books. They appreciate my trying ... but I don't think I'll do as well learning phrases as I usually do. My hearing loss makes a difference.

On August 2, a student and I will go to his village by a four-hour bus trip where I'll preach through an interpreter.

It pours down rain almost every day and there is thunder and lightning with it (which I enjoy). The weather is very hot and very humid with all that comes with that kind of weather. The campus looks like a former missionary compound with swampy terrain. Bananas hang on their big leafy trees, palms and coconuts are prevalent. I wash from a bucket and sleep in the "guest house." The seminary provides a cook for me so I eat rice, chicken, and real Indonesian food twice a day.

I'm not at all sure what I'll do after the three week intensive is over. I may stay here and offer a course for pastors on discipling or

I may teach in the continuing ed. program at the Batak Church headquarters. There is also the request for a women's Bible School visit. In the midst of ants, mosquitoes, crowing roosters, and devout Christians, I send my love.

This Sunday has been an interesting one. After my last class on Saturday, a student and I caught a little twelve-seat bus with seventeen in it (plus merchandise and farm produce) and rode to Lake Toba in the middle of Sumatra. He and I caught a ferry at Parapat and rode to an island called Samosir where we stayed over one night at a village named Tuk-Tuk. One of these ferries capsized last week and 89 were drowned. Many were Batak who trace their roots back to this island. The buildings have the upswept ends which is the typical Batak architectural style. This a.m. we caught the boat back and worshipped in a Batak church. This is a vital and alive church of nearly 3,000 congregations in Indonesia with a real shortage of pastors. Many of the present clergy have six to nine preaching points in addition to their main congregation making up the parish.

Tuk-Tuk Village
Lake Toba on Samosir Island

This late afternoon I had a little victory as one of my students brought her family to meet me and she introduced them

12

in English! She and I were both so pleased. The students have asked to start a discussion group in my house on theology (in English) — great!

For a while I had one class convinced that my hearing aid was an "Indonesian translator" — and another class that it picked up "student whispers."

I washed out some clothing in a bucket tonight. I'm not sure I'll ever get the knack of bathing with a bucket and dipper ... but cool water on my skin in any way I can manage helps with the humid heat.

A new baby was born in the house next to mine last Sunday night. No doctor or mid-wife, just the mother and father-in-law to help with delivery. That's managed care!

After ten days, I'd say the Batak are a short, square, solid people with black hair and a gentle sense of humor. They are very polite and somewhat timid, and seem very resolved to their fate in life. They're loving and appreciative of any effort made on their behalf. They love music. Their religion shows German Protestant influence still. Several clergy wear the German Geneva gown and white preaching tabs.

I'm not sure my students are, but I'm learning a lot about a marvelous culture and a particular practice of Christianity I knew so little about.

July 28, 1997
Dear Friends and Family,

I have just finished teaching during a rainstorm while the roof leaked all over the place. The students don't seem to notice.

My residence is quite a place! There are chickens everywhere including two roosters who wake me about the same time as the Muslim call to worship (4:30 a.m.). I also have geese, a pond, and a swamp beside my house to keep the mosquitoes breeding. A family of musangs (wildcats/civits) live between the ceiling and roof. And Saturday when I came to my front door in the morning, there was a cobra snake about six feet long trying to get under my front door. The house is full of termites which have eaten away much of the superstructure. Of course there are ants everywhere including on my eating table. This past weekend there was no electricity and no water (still no water today). There is lush jungle all around: fruits such as banana, mango, duran, pineapple everywhere.

This past weekend I took a trip by bus and boat to Parapat village and boat to Samosir Island (second one) where I rented a motorcycle (with international driver's license) and rode it to Tomok, burial place of early Sumatra Kings including one baptized by Ludwig Nommensen, a Dane sent by the Germans, which was the beginning of Lutheran Batak and Christian religion here in the 1860s. Nommensen remained here until his death in 1918 serving the Batak Church (now 3,000 congregations) for 56 years.

From 1940 when the Japanese occupied the island and interned all the Germans, the Batak Church has been independent. It has been a part of the Lutheran World Federation since 1953 with its own confession. Ludwig Nommensen is still called "the Apostle to the Batak." The first training school for Batak evangelists was established in 1868.

There is an "adat" (unwritten code or law) among Batak. It requires a "Buis" which metes out punishment for breaking the adat. Remnants of animism exist like belief in the "begu" (ghost). I attended a Hula Hula Sunday afternoon. A baby boy had been born next door to the Naingolans. The community came for a feast and speeches with the food provided by the wife's family called

Hula Hula. The man's side (Baru) has certain responsibilities also. I ate sac-sang which is a mixture of pork and blood. No silverware. I've had to get accustomed to eating with my fingers like the rest of Indonesians. By the way, they do still eat dog!

On the bus trip across Sumatra I saw many rice farmers, water buffalo, and the beautiful Batak buildings (Rumah Batak). They are harvesting and drying the rice on the ground.

I have now seen the famous dance "Si Gale Gale." Mostly done with the fingers and hands.

My daily schedule goes like this: up very early with coffee I make. Wash with a dipper and bucket (when I have water). Preach or worship at 7:30 a.m. with students. Teach from 8 to 9:40 a.m. and 10 to 11:40. A cook has a meal for me at noon, followed by a nap during the very hot time of day. Teach again at 2:30 p.m. until 4:10. Then a Bentang Bier at my house and dinner about 6:00. Listen to BBC from 7 to 8:00 p.m. Prepare for the next day's teaching. Rinse from a bucket if I have water, and to bed by 10:00 p.m.

I kicked out a student for cheating and it has caused a serious confusion. Penipu = cheat. The students have a habit of cheating in the villages and all do it. Several students came to me to "beg mercy" so I let him back in. That class has been *very* well behaved since then. Today I was so proud as one class told in English of their weekend, history of Sumatra, news from the local newspaper, etc.

Today the authorities shot a woman caught smuggling drugs at Medan airport. She was caught two days ago. Swift justice!!

This is not the rainy season, but it rains a lot and that gives some relief from humidity. These buildings were built by the German missionaries and now are badly deteriorating. Mold, lack of any maintenance, cultural differences in life style, and the termites are destroying the campus.

To ride the bus somewhere is a real experience. Saturday I took a bus which had all sorts of stuff, living and dead, on top with five of us in a seat built for three (with a sick girl throwing up). The aisles were full of people who fall on one another when the driver goes around a corner, always honking the horn to scare the animals and people off the narrow road, with loud music playing and most

15

of the men smoking one cigarette after another. No schedule, just the first ones on and off we go ... but it's cheap!

I will travel every weekend now to preach in rural villages except August 17 (their independence day) when I will preach at the Cathedral Church here in Siantar. I will finish teaching English next Saturday and then will do some lectures in discipling and many in homiletics.

Sometimes I walk, sometimes take a "becak" (motorcycle with a sidecar); but most times I ride in a pick-up truck converted to a bus. The Toba Batak are beautiful people, short, dark, black hair, athletic, thick hips and shallow breasted, with a wonderful sparkle in their black eyes. They are gracious to others, confident that God is eager to assist, not being overly sensitive to their faults. Today there must be more than three million Christians in Batakland. They possess great self-confidence, great zeal, and great ambition, not sure they are Reformed or Lutheran or Catholic. They are always themselves.

Muslim people have all the high positions. In Indonesia 85% are Muslim, 6.3% Christian, and 2% Hindu-Bali. There are both "ethnic" and "gathered" churches. There are five distinct groups of Bataks closely related ethnically, but having some language difference.

Sumatra's Proleptic Calm
Before Sumatra's sultry sunset
sudden stillness comes
a pregnant cosmic pause:
dog's barking stops
rooster crows no more
muted is honk of geese
the wind lays still and
humidity presses heavy
banana leaves refuse to rattle
Muslim call to prayer surceases

16

There is proleptic calm
for reflection and breath taking
the earth waits in anticipation
day's creatures are weary
night's not yet in motion
Then life begins anew
little creatures stir
Beginning evening's melodies
the musang commences prowl
routine has its way once more.

— JLS

August 4, 1997
Dear Friends and Family,

Salamat Padi, in Indonesian: good morning!

It's Monday morning and I am taking it easy after three weeks of intensive teaching and a weekend trip back into Sumatra's jungle.

I am learning so much about the Batak culture. After riding a country bus over terrible roads for three hours, I walked into the bush for about three miles. Three students went with me to this "Bona ni Pinasa" (village of origin). It is a village of about 200 who own the land together with mainly two family surnames (Sinaga). The people there farm rice and coffee and a little corn and also raise for meat pigs, chickens, pigeons, and dogs. It was harvest time and they had cut the rice and were beating it on boards to shuck it. Then the chaff is burned and the ashes spread on the fields for fertilizer. Water buffalo help with the replanting. The coffee beans were also being picked, hulled, dried, and ground into fine flour so all they need do is roast and add hot water.

Batak women in Tapiannauli on their way to a Hula Hula
with gifts of rice on their heads.

Sinaga family in village of Tapiannuali Sumatra
Deonal in center; Guru father is a teacher; mother is a farmer

We stayed in the house of my student whose family gave me a fine room and bed; all the rest slept on mats on the floor. An attached cook-shack with wood fire and lots of smoke was the kitchen. We bathed with a dipper and bucket with rain water (their only

A Karo Batak woman
The Batak subgroups are Karo, Toba, Simalungun,
AngKolo, Mandailing, and Pakpak/Dairi

water supply unless they walk a half to three-quarter mile to a stream).

The Batak Lutheran Church is there (HKBP — Huria Kristen Batak Protestan) where I taught about 150 Saturday evening and preached with one of my students interpreting to about 200 Sunday morning. Men sit on one side, women in their beautiful Kebayas (skirts) on the other, children in yet another section ... and how they do sing the hymns in Batak to German and English hymn-tunes. All the older women wore old-fashioned corsets (!) just under their blouse and Kebaya, easily observed. I have no idea why; but I suspect some German missionary of long ago told them they must for church! While still in the pews after the liturgy, the men light up tobacco and the old women chew a red substance called napuran. They made some speeches and presented me with a beautiful ulas, a piece of cloth that Batak wear over the right shoulder which is also used in the wedding ceremony to wrap around the bride and groom. It is my third ulas!

After worship they held a Hula Hula in my honor. They had killed a pig and fixed the heart for me. The rest they made into "sac-sang" which is meat, fat, and blood cooked together with very

A celebration (Hula Hula) in the Sinaga home

21

hot spices (remember this is "spice island!"). We all sat cross-legged on mats with no utensils at all and ate with our fingers. A bowl of rain water is near for washing the hand as we eat. One soon gets the hang of balling up the rice with whatever and getting it to the mouth! The village name is Tapiannauli.

There is a "teacher" (Pandita) who has cared for this village's congregation for 22 years. I was told that I was the first American ever to visit there. The mother congregation, about ten miles away, has seven other preaching points and their one pastor. The chief-for-life of the village has a nurse stationed in his home and I think paid for by the government of Indonesia. She also provides family planning for the village.

While many are very poor in Sumatra, they all seem to have enough to eat. But life in a little village must be very hard, especially for the women.

To this date I have not been at all ill. I don't expect to lose any weight, as my cook prepares fine food, and I drink considerable beer which is safe, good, and cheap.

My students had a "Hula Hula" for me the last class session and presented me with a fountain pen set. They then sang and both men and women danced the "Si Gale Gale." They loved it that I tried to dance with them. Many cried. Several gave me their little treasures like a tiny New Testament. It was very moving. We made so much noise, reaching some fervor in the dancing that the whole seminary came to see.

I'm preaching often now. I was the preacher at the closing of the summer school Saturday morning. Then I preached Saturday night and Sunday morning in Tapiannauli. It's an excellent opportunity to explore cross-cultural preaching. In a celebration recently, I learned that the Batak often respond with "Ima-tu-tu" which means "May it be true." So Saturday's theme was "Ima-tu-tu According to Mark." They loved it and appreciate any way I try to include their culture in the sermon. To do narrative is very difficult until I get more experience here. Stories or humor from my culture don't communicate. The death of a faculty's daughter last week gave me one more narrative possibility.

Five third-year students just paid me a visit and asked that I teach in their homiletics class. I'll meet the lecturer tonight and make plans to do so.

Later today I'll do my washing and place it out on some bushes to dry in this strong sun. Many will parade by to see what the American wears.

I have converted an old water tank from the guest house into a bath tub of sorts and am much more comfortable as I can climb into it and the cool rain water helps. It's much better than the squat position and a bucket and dipper.

Sorry to ramble, but conciseness and focus is much more difficult in this climate. I'm so glad I came, for these Batak are very special "Lutherans" I'll always cherish. The little inconveniences are nothing to the strength and beauty of Sumatrans.

"Pantum gangoluan, tois bamagoan" — Batak for "Courteousness is life; impudence is ruin."

As the time of my service as a volunteer missionary in Indonesia (the fifth largest country by population in the world right behind the U.S.) runs out, I write you this final report and observations.

As I finished teaching the three-week intensive English course to sixty entering students, the advanced students returned. I then began to lecture on homiletics, stewardship, evangelism, and discipleship which are comparatively new subjects to be considered here. At night the students would gather in bunches of six to sixteen at my home to discuss my lectures in English, sing by guitar, and drink tea.

I attended my third Hula Hula (a celebration ceremony with much formality and too many speeches!) to celebrate the pregnancy of one of the faculty wives. We were served pork and blood cooked with much spice (sac-sang), goldfish, and rice — all eaten by hand while seated cross-legged on the beautifully matted floor. As the honored guest, again I got the pig's head and heart. (I learned quickly to share this with the elders.)

A trip last week with an interpreter in the principal's car took me to the Teacher/Preacher School where I lectured for three hours to about 110. I stayed at the Bible Women's School in a class room with a sheet on a wire for privacy, lecturing there for another three hours, preaching in chapel, and meeting with faculty. In each institution there are about 110 students preparing for their specific roles as pastor's helper in a parish of many preaching points. They spend three years getting ready for their calling.

My driver also took me to historic spots, such as the place of burial of the "Apostle to the Bataks," that of Ludwig Nommensen, a Dane sent by the German Rhenish Church, a mile hike up a mountain to Peace Cross overlooking Taratung and its little village square. In 1865 the Bataks tried to kill Nommensen for purchasing slaves and setting them free to become Christians. Before that in 1834 two missionaries from the U.S. were killed and eaten by the Bataks

24

Ludwig Ingwer Nommensen's tugn where he is buried.
North of Logabodi and south end of Lake Toba

giving them their first real taste of religion! I photographed a memorial to this feast and the old caretaker remarked that he had in him "American missionary blood, as my ancestors had eaten at least two!"

I preached at the HKBP church headquarters and met staff where I continually was asked why the LWF in July only recognized the former Bishop who was voted out of office in 1993 and has started his own seminary. He is still ordaining and trying to be Bishop. The military helped in that '93 election, not uncommon here, where church and government is all intertwined. The interns in the area spent the evening discussing their ministries and some political and religious issues with me.

On my last Sunday, the present Bishop invited me to take part in an ordination service in Medan. The two of us led a procession of about 500 through town to the church. A sixteen piece band went ahead of us. I preached and spoke, bringing greetings from ELCA Presiding Bishop H. George Anderson and the DGM secretary, Warner Luoma. The service took a little over four hours and we ordained twelve Bible women, one deaconess, and twenty-eight teacher/preachers. They also sometimes ordain elders, pastors, and evangelists. There is a laying on of hands only by the Bishop except when pastors join in ordaining other pastors. After the service there were eight speeches and then all 500 ate sac-sang, rice, and goldfish. This took place in the sanctuary with the Bishop and myself as honored guests in the front row eating with our hands and getting the head and tail of the pig and goldfish. It was a fine celebration. I knew enough Batak by then to lace my words with their idioms, which they loved.

Sunday evening I visited Nommensen University in Medan, drank beer with the seminary principal, and ate pizza at a just-opened Pizza Hut. On Monday, I depart this Batakland and the people I have come to love.

Farewells were awkward for me to express to these modest and shy people who do not hug. We just shook hands making the traditional hand touch to the chest over the heart and let the tears flow. All sorts of ulas, little souvenirs, and tapes of their own singing with guitar were handed to me to take home, so I do not forget them. We prayed often and touched our hearts again and again.

Probably my greatest contributions over these past eight weeks were helping a brand new teacher of homiletics organize his course and to prepare a recent graduate to lecture on discipleship using my copied notes.

But our Christian lives have touched and we have shared cultures, food, music, grieving, and celebrations. I have yet another people I have come to love.

Rupinna Br. Panggabean preparing the meal in the Sinaga home

Batak Village Woman
Before dawn on Sriwijaya's empire
at boldest rooster's shrill crow
the resolute Batak village woman
rises from her nocturnal modom.

From a blue plastic bucket
she bathes her golden brown skin
with Toba's cool rainwater
preparing for long day's labor.

Si Raja Batak's strong daughter
with high cheek bones, square jaw
and narrow sparkling Sumatran eyes
is graced by long black hair glistening.

Short and sturdy of Indonesia stature
with loin-producing valued sons
and shallow breast for suckle
her seldom words are certain.

The kebaya is arranged discreetly
as deep lines in majestic face
betray a toilsome life's existence
of farmer, wife, and many's mother.

She lives by the Batak adat
and faith in Nommensen's Jesus
from Bona ni Pinasa's dawn to dark
sweltering labor on island: singing.

— JLS

(Published in *A Celebration of Poets*, 1998)

Batak Tugu on Samosir Island — Sumatra

Summer Sojourn in Argentina, Uruguay, and Suriname

July, 1998
Dear Friends and Family,

Greetings from the land of maté and "más o menos"! (More or less — a favorite saying of most Uruguayans.) The flight from SFO and then Miami to Buenos Aires was good with only ten minutes at the Miami airport to make the connecting flight.

I was met in Argentina by the President of IELU (United Evangelical Lutheran Church) in whose home I also stayed while lecturing and preaching: the Rev. Angel Furlan. I have established a real friendship with him and his wife Isabel.

ISEDET is the result of a merger of our Lutheran Seminary and seven other demoninations: 150 students, sixteen faculty. All students work during the day. All classes are held at night. I lectured to students and faculty in the mornings and laity in the afternoons. One half of the facilities are rented to a small university in order to have desperately needed income.

One afternoon and evening I spent with an old friend, Rev. Ricardo Pietroantonio, professor and former president of the church and of the seminary. He is writing a three-volume history of Lutheranism in Argentina and Uruguay. He was fascinated with my small rememberances of information about missionary Rev. John Armbruster, friend of my family, from my Greenville home congregation. Ricardo seemed so hungry for friendship and for serious theological reflection. I learned much.

Today I saw the grave of Eva Perón and the Casa Rosada where they ruled and spoke. It was a moving experience to see the "Madres de Plaza de Mayo" where the mothers of many sons missing from the time of military repression protest.

It's winter and that means much rain, mud, and very cool temperatures. Northern Argentina is warmer.

29

Pastor Raul Denuncio, Beatriz (Betty) Simonassi de Farré, and I flew from Buenos Aires up country to Posada, rode in a borrowed car to Missiones District to the border of Paraguay to see the beautiful Iguazú Falls on the Paraná where *The Mission* was filmed. I also visited the home of famous Uruguayan poet and author, Horacio Quiroga, and the Jesuit ruins of San Ignatio nearby.

We then moved to the El Dorado town where a group of Germans are very conflicted in their little church. I couldn't see that we helped very much. I learned to eat "manioca" (like a potato) there. One can still see a few Gruta people native to Argentina.

The next three nights we stayed in a pension in the town of Oberá. My work was to preach at this Swedish background Olas Petri Lutheran Church and to work with some laity on discipling and coping with loss and grief. The Rev. Juana Corigliano (a woman who is the former President of IELU) is the senior pastor. Work began here years ago by Swedish missionaries because of the many Swedes immigrating through Brazil. It is a gently rolling country

Olas Petri Lutheran Church, Oberá, N. Argentina. Pastor Juana Corigliano, former President of the Lutheran Church of Argentina is fifth from the left. Dr. Schmalenberger is eighth from left. After worship.

near Brazil and the rain forest where the main work is logging and lumber. At my workshop on witnessing, there was an old man who was baptized by Rev. Herman Hammer and confirmed by John Armbruster! I worked with the council in breaking out of their passive mode. Mission statements and strategic planning seem foreign, but they are going to try. My modeling of speaking about Jesus out loud and praying seemed a welcome surprise.

The beautiful ministry here is out in the colonies where Pastor Julio Ross moves through the red mud on horrible roads to visit and conduct worship using guitar. I drank "maté" (yerba tea) with very poor families in their small houses built on the twenty acres of land given to them by the government during the military rule in Argentina. When a son marries, the farm must be divided and thus they become poorer and poorer. They loved to speak German with me. Most of their parents came from Germany, Denmark, or Sweden. They are gauchos without the traditional outfits. It is a simple, hard life worshipping twice a month in a tin-roof, handmade brick church built with their own hands. The bricks are hand made from the red clay soil along the road. We often held hands and prayed.

At Oberá, when I preached, the wealthy and these poor, who are their servants during the week, sat side by side.

We visited the owner of a "yerba" (the leaf for the maté) factory where they dry this plant, chop, and package it for consumption. It is a very important liturgy of friendship for Argentinians and even more so for Uruguayans. The hot water is poured from a thermos over the gourd full of the tea leaves with a silver straw/ strainer. This is passed from person to person. Filling stations have hot water dispensers for maté.

The daily schedule seems to be: get up late and have coffee and milk. Maté mid-morning. Lunch as a big meal about noon. Maté and snack about 4 or 5 p.m. and the big meal of the day at 9:30 or 10:00 p.m.! In several larger towns there were restaurants which didn't even open for business until 9:00 p.m.

31

Beatriz S. de Farré filling her thermos with hot water

So much kissing! It says "hello" and "good-bye" — in the north on each cheek, in the south just on the left cheek.

Many of these Lutheran congregations were started about forty or fifty years ago. The Lutheran Church in America reduced financial support 10% a year from 1970 to 1980, then moved to a different partnership of providing some support for approved projects.

We spent a day in Posada. It is very German. Many former Nazis there. The pastor is one who was tortured in Chile and who Bishop Helmut Frentz and then President of IELU, Juan Cobrda, helped escape to Argentina. He is a socialist in the midst of this very pro-German community. Many immigrated here after WWII. Nazi sympathizers are still very strong. The congregation includes a parochial school and a girls' boarding dorm for those going to the University. It was fun talking with them — it's called the Gutenberg Institute. I was relieved I did not hear of any of my relatives dwelling there.

We then flew back to Buenos Aires and on to Montevideo. I lectured at the Ecumenical Institute and at the Lutheran Center

The Lutheran Center, Montevideo, Uruguay

where Raul Denuncio is director and pastor of the little thirty-member Lutheran congregation. Our foster daughter, Betty Simonassi de Farré, holds the whole thing together and has done so ever since returning from our Ohio home. We can be very, very proud of her. I spent the morning at the congregation's mission in a slum of Montevideo. There a couple have permitted a small chapel to be built next to their home where the government parcels out the lots and people build the house. Pastor Denuncio put on the zinc roof with his own hands. During the week, it serves as a child care center and early Sunday it is their church. Between fifteen and thirty attend. In the last four years eighty have been baptized. Sunday School is Sunday afternoon. The poor and little children have a very special place in God's sight, I'm sure!

I am so surprised about how people are very ethnicity-conscious (and race as well) in Argentina. That brings me to my visit to the Montevideo Rotary Club. Wow! The meeting started at 9:00 p.m. (really 9:35). The meal was chicken cutlet, french fries, fried banana, and good beer with 24 men in attendance. An intense discussion followed about whether to receive women or "negros" into

33

the club. Then, I was surprised to hear myself introduced as the program for the evening at 10:30 p.m. I spoke about what a joy it was to be inclusive in our culture, my own life, and even the Rotary. The discussion which followed was interesting and memorable. Some younger members afterwards said how thrilled they were to have a speaker with an "open mind." Others left grumbling to each other.

What a joy it is to stay with Betty and her family. Antonio Farré (her husband) uses his engineering skills as the maintenance and housekeeping supervisor at a private hospital where his sister is a doctor (as is her husband). In order to accommodate me, all three children sleep in one small room and I sleep in Tamara's (seventeen) room. They are wonderful kids and we have bonded in a great "Grandpa love." They also installed a modern bathroom just before my arrival. Diego is thirteen and Damian is fifteen. The night before I left, we went to see and hear tango and gaucho and carnival dancing in which we all took part. Tamara wants to visit us for a term at Los Medanos "like Mommie did." The house is heated with a couple of wood-burning stoves. It is a poorer end of

Antonio Farré and his children

34

town where garbage piles up in the street and the smell of sewage is strong. They keep a couple of German shepherds to protect the house which was completely looted about one year ago. Betty has great respect throughout the Lutheran Church. An excellent translator, I think! All three kids make excellent grades.

Tuesday morning I went with Tamara to her English class and talked with them for an hour and a half. It was a chance to explain Lutheranism in a country which is so secular and Roman Catholic. They can't imagine a priest who is married and surely not a woman priest either!

We ate dinner one night at Antonio's sister and brother-in-law's home. Both are medical doctors. His son was one of the two survivors of the Rugby team which crashed in the Andes, who walked out for help. Betty's second job is to take the bills of these two doctors personally to the homes of the patients and then pick up the money. Checks and mail are not used in Uruguay or many third world countries.

I preached at the only IELU congregation in Uruguay on Sunday morning. It's a lively worship. A man of 65 years, the pastor gathers the little flock of perhaps twenty to thirty. Comments about my sermon were "it was very human." One young woman came because she read in her history class about the Reformation, has studied my book, and is now confirmed. After a big Sunday lunch, we danced and danced. Betty's two sisters were there.

This thought comes from Walter Altmann: "The Pentecostal Church is the only religious group I have seen that really has managed to accompany these millions of Latin American poor who have migrated during the last few decades. It holds a liberating potential." It seems that throughout Latin American history, the church has been predominantly an instrument of domination. It has presented a Jesus of history and ethnic tradition and not of presence with us now.

It's crucial to understand that our life under grace not be understood as an individualistic life, just an inner peace, perhaps, but rather a collective community life that takes concrete form in our cultures.

35

It took two cars to go to the airport for my departure. Two of Tamara's friends, who sometimes slept here and spoke English with me every chance they got, had to go along with Denuncio, Tamara, and Diego. All cried, but especially Tamara and Betty. I think loving friendships are more intense under these kinds of circumstances — distance and limited time.

United Airlines cancelled its flight from Montevideo to Buenos Aires, so they put me on a little local flight (with smoking). As we taxied out, we very nearly missed a collision with another plane taxying in. The brakes were slammed on and everyone was thrown into the seat ahead. I shouted, "Look out," while looking out the window (as if that would help). It really shook up a lot of the passengers.

After two weeks it occurs to me how sweet homecoming will be!

P.S. The microwaves in appliance stores have a setting listed as "más/menos"! (more or less)

Evil's Progeny

Through some mysterious demonic strategy
the winter's caustic fog of race hatred obscures
with a cloudy swastica the scourged Savior
impaled there by evil's venom progeny.
Neither the poignant taste of yerba mate
nor rusty deluge can wash away its infection.

The Nazi brown pollutes our baptism water
and thanksgiving sacrament's potential potency,
the God of Argentina's red clay grieves
before liturgical false vacuous contrition.

— JLS

Suriname, Humanity's Mixing Bowl

Greetings from Suriname. I arrived two days late as my flight from Curaçao to Suriname was cancelled and I had to stay there two nights.

I'm staying with Lucretia von Ommeren, former PLTS student (who works so hard to make me comfortable), her sister, and her niece whose name is Heaven. Members of the congregation bring food to help them with my visit.

There is a wonderful connection between the Javanese here and those in Indonesia — same food, culture, language, customs. This is part of Lucretia's heritage also.

The Rev. Lucretia von Ommeren

With my German I can understand some of the Dutch which is the official language. The buildings and culture reflect strongly the Dutch colonization. I do get some words from the native language ("Sarangatang tongo") from my Indonesian Batak vocabulary.

It is very hot and rains a couple of times a day. The people are a beautiful mixture of Creoles (descendants of ex-slaves and African descent), Hindustanis, Javanese, Bush Negros (known as Maroons), Amerindians, Jews, Lebanese, Dutch, and a few Europeans. Bauxite is a big industry.

The people seem so appreciative of my teaching. I am learning and sharing so much so far: led a retreat of council members, preached at Lucretia's mission congregation in the housing project of Paramaribo, have taught a couple of sessions on Discipleship at the mother church. They are keeping me busy elsewhere too — I delivered lectures on preaching and evangelism at the Moravian Seminary in Paramaribo and attended a Pentecostal pastor's installation as Bible Society leader.

I look forward to next Monday with the pastors of many denominations. On this Sunday I'll preach at the Maarten Luther Kerk in Paramaribo.

Moravian Seminary in Paramaribo

38

It is a real joy to see Lucretia do her ministry and to see the respect she enjoys here. In visiting a hospital with "Domine Lucretia," the mix of Hindu, Muslim, and Christian was an interesting challenge in pastoral care and theology.

I anticipate my homecoming after many weeks away!

Peace On Curaçao

There is a mystic time span
before night's black darkness
when peace to all is breathed
and waves repeat the incantation.

The ocean breeze gently caresses
those who pause to feel it.
A half Caribbean silver moon
hangs the calm word aloft.

Clouds write it in the heavens,
the soft palm rattle adds rhythm
and from the aquatic fog,
those present are mist annointed.

The horizon merges sky and ocean.
Quiet reigns like Curaçao's humidity.
The steel drums celebrate its presence,
a purple whisper is deeply inhaled.

— JLS

(Curaçao is an island in the Caribbean near Suriname)

In Suriname there are five ordained Lutheran clergy (with two inactive): Pearl Gerding at the Maarten Luther Kerk (which is the mother church, better than 250 years old); a young man, Michael Stewart, at both Bethlehemkerk and a mission, Pauluskerk, re-starting after struggling for thirty years; and Lucretia van Ommeren, who is establishing the mission in the housing projects called Gemeenschap van Hoop. All three active clergy got their education at the Theological College of the West Indies in Jamaica.

I have learned of Lucretia's involvement with the mothers of missing sons and husbands. Like the mothers in Argentina, they protest on the square close to where Lucretia was pastor. She gave them food and provided toilets at the church in defiance of the rather unstable government and some in her congregation.

A full schedule finished up my time there:

Friday — Resumed my lectures at Maarten Luther Kerk doing actual witness instruction for the laity and clergy. (This was all new to them and they loved it!)

Rev. Lucretia von Ommeren's home where she grew up

Saturday — Led an all day session on stewardship and evangelism for an ecumenical group at a Roman Catholic retreat center. Sunday — Preached at Bethlehem Kerk and then to Maarten Luther Kerk to preach there. I met with the parish council at their request, who wanted some advice on several clergy problems.

In the evening we attended a Javanese "Verjari," which is Sarangatang Tongo for "celebration" of the 65th birthday of Lucretia's father with lots of food and family. It was held where Lucretia grew up "when it was all bush and full of animals, including many monkeys." We danced in the mud, celebrated and generally fed the mosquitos in this lower-than-sea-level swampland.

On Monday evening I lectured to the pastors on homiletics at the request of the parish council. On Tuesday Lucretia arranged a visit to the American Embassy where her friend gave us a great tour at its tightened security, as there are offshore and onshore oil reserves to be protected here as well. That evening I conducted a house blessing for Pastor von Ommeren with the Lutherans of Paramaribo surprising me with a "slamatan" in my honor to say good-bye. This means food, pork, beer, satay (barbequed meat on a stick), rice, and plantain chips (similar to unsweet bananas) late into the night. Several hours of sleep and then rising at 3 a.m. for flights: Paramaribo, Curaçao, Miami, Chicago, and on to San Francisco.

I am so thankful today for such rich memories and wonderful new friends. I hope I made a little contribution to the people I worked with. Homecoming is great! The farewells were sorrowful and significant.

Kwakoe — freedom fighter in downtown Paramaribo

Paramaribo's Kwakoe
In humid day light the smooth ebony statue
stands erect to show Maroons their slave chains
to passers-by who casual-glance his direction
for a reminder of slavery's cruel days on plantations.

But in the darkest night-time of Paramaribo city
when the merchants' iron gates are locked securely
and garbage strewn brick walks are ghostly vacant,
the rigid shiny Kwakoe slowly lives and kneels.

From eyes which cannot close for nocturnal rest
there secretes from absent salty tear glands
ghostly signs of inhumanity's anguish over Suriname.
No one comes to wipe anguished tears or balm the sore pain.

As dawn's first light sneaks around Dutch buildings
before slaves' children caressed by raven silky hair
disregard the memorial to their freedom fighter,
knees straighten, cheeks dry, and hope comes for recognition.

— JLS

(Kwakoe is the statue of a rebel slave freedom fighter)

43

Faxes from Neuendettlesau, Germany

I arrived early at Nürnberg and so had a bratwurst while waiting for Professor Riess. We drove through several Franconian villages before arriving at Neuendettelsau. We ate Friday evening dinner in a Gasthof Keim. Beer and schnitzel — such good food! — although today I got at the vegetarian table here at the Hochschule. Ugh!

The farmers come into this town on Friday night and play cards at Gasthof Keim — a noisy bunch, but what fun. Herr Keim and I communicate in German as best we can and are developing a friendship. It's a short walk to his place from my room in the dorm.

Saturday I walked around the village finding Wilhelm Loehe's St. Nicholai Church, his home, hospital, mission office, Diakonia school, and retirement home. The students at the seminary know little about him. They are much more worried about passing their Greek, Hebrew, and Latin. *(Wilhelm Löhe — Loehe in English — sent German pastors to frontier American seminaries to learn English for becoming German-speaking pastors to the German immigrants, primarily in Ohio, Indiana, Iowa, Michigan, and other midwestern states.)*

I find that the Ft. Wayne Seminary was signed over to the Missouri Synod. It originally was begun by Löhe's men from Neuendettelsau. He also seems to be the Patron Saint of Wartburg in Dubuque. Jim Schaaf's *(history professor at Trinity Seminary)* book is very helpful in trying to understand this place and its theology of the church. What I have read to this date surely explains how Schmucker and the "new measure men" were a real threat to the disciples of Löhe. No wonder Wittenberg College sprang up in Ohio! *(Begun by Gettysburg Seminary graduates, disciples of Schmucker, in Springfield, Ohio, as an English speaking institution since Capital in Columbus taught only in German.)*

Preaching Assumptions of Wilhelm Löhe

1. The preacher turns to the church as the community of Jesus Christ which continually lives in communion with the redeemer.
2. It is the confession and witness of the Christian community which enjoys a lively relationship with Christ and which, through the preacher, brings this relationship to expression in representative communication.
3. He bound together the Christian and the human, the gospel, and the concrete life.
4. The fourth typical aspect is his molding of the sermon into a work of art ... the shaping of the sermon according to the rules of content and style in rhetoric.

Today I attended church at St. Nicholai. They still use the black robe and white preaching tabs. The nave is well appointed with a large crucifix behind the altar and the pastor facing the crucifix while chanting most of the service. The traditional high-in-the-air pulpit is used, as is the sign of the cross, and, of course, kneelers. There were about 150-200 in church. While I did not know many of the words, I easily recognized the liturgy and delighted in taking communion. Pastor Walter invited me to come visit so we could talk about Löhe and also about parish ministry now.

The students are mainly from Bavaria, and we are having a good time getting to know each other as we eat together in the dining hall three times a day. A couple of them have cars and have offered to transport me when I need it. There is a little three-car train which runs between these Franconian villages and peeps a shrill horn as it arrives in Neuendettelsau frequently. I can take it to Ansbach and then get a larger train to anywhere I want to go.

I don't plan to travel for a while as I have a cold and want to get my *Preparation For Discipleship* manuscript well underway. I also want to write some verses about this village, Wittenberg, and Schmalenberg. Perhaps when I get rested up from the tour, that will come easier.

There is no TV available here. I brought along my little short-wave and get the news at 9 p.m. over BBC. The inter-campus phone does not connect to outside lines. I'm hoping it will be warmer in my dorm room when the students return in another week.

I have a desk in the library which I'll enjoy as my work place. I've yet to develop a routine, but it will probably entail a long walk in the early morning, working on my manuscript till lunch, a nap, some searching for Löhe places and things, visiting the various institutions and people, dinner with the students, and perhaps a little fellowship with my new friends at the Gasthof Keim.

These words leaped off the page today:

"For the lonely man, all the treasures of the world are no substitute for companionship. Narrower than a prison is the wide earth to an abandoned and lonely man ...

Behold the Church! It is the very opposite of loneliness — blessed fellowship! There are millions of saints and believers who are blessed in it. No longer lonely, but filled, satisfied, yes, blessed ..." (Wilhelm Löhe).

For lunch in the dorm today we had longwurst, sauerkraut, potatoes, and kükle — the students said a typical meal here. I'll probably look like St. Nicholas by his day in December.

This has been quite an experience. This little seminary called Augustana-Hochschule is located near Nürnburg on the site where there was formerly an ammunition factory during World War II. The factory was built in the trees among the many institutional buildings to keep the Allies from bombing. The archivist here told me the truth and admitted that many of the retarded and ill were taken to the gas chambers — and with the cooperation of the Director.

The Augustana Hochschule

These institutions of mercy are the plowshares of that history in the legacy of Wilhelm Löehe in this town where he began the Inner Mission work, deaconess movement, homes for orphans, aged, mentally disadvantaged, and others. I worshipped this morning with nearly 200 retired "Krankenhaus" sisters (health care) in their traditional white hats and black clothing. A hundred others work in the local institutions. They ride bicycles everywhere!

I have spent much time in the archives researching Löehe's life, work, and preaching style. It turns out that he was known as

A monument to the many children
taken to the gas chambers by the Nazis

one of the greatest preachers of his time. He is famous in the U.S. as the father of our Wartburg Seminary in addition to his work in Ft. Wayne.

Next week I'll spend time in the home of the just retired pastor of the Stadtkirche in Wittenberg. He had been pastor there for thirty years and we have visited several times before. I'll preach there on Sunday and visit Möhra, home and burial place of Katherine von Bora.

Writing is going well. I have a first draft of a 100-page new member book completed: *Preparation For Discipleship.* I've completed a camera-ready collection of 55 poems and pictures ready to publish for family members when I get back.

I'm now doing something I have saved up for a long time — organizing by categories and writing out in full the narratives and metaphors I have journaled in my homiletical journals. There will be about 500 of them. Titled *These Will Preach*, CSS will publish just as soon as I can get the manuscript completed. I think I remember a few hunting stories which will no doubt make my friends famous!

This is really Bavaria, Germany! The food and beer are wonderful. The dining hall at this school serves a full menu: dumplings, noodles, all sorts of wurst, soups, cakes, pastries. It's like going to a German restaurant every lunch and dinner. The school has its own bar open on Wednesday evenings.

Hochschule students at their campus bar

49

Nov 17, 1996
Dear Friends and Family,

I have just last night returned from my week in Wittenberg.
While there, the Synod was meeting so I was able to meet many
clergy. Pastor Hasse and wife are such gracious hosts! There was a
reunion of those active in the movement to bring down the Berlin
wall from both Berlin and Wittenberg.

Church doors at Wittenberg
where 95 Thesis were posted by Martin Luther

We drove one day to Torgau so I could visit where Katie Luther died, is buried, and where Luther traveled more than 41 times. He also consecrated the first Lutheran Church there. I spent Saturday with Eckhard Naumann (Lord High Mayor of Wittenberg) and Ulrich Pfingsten (Minister of Culture) at a concert in the Stadtkirche — Brahms' *Requeim*. On the return trip I went again to Eisenach, hired a taxi, and drove to Möhra, where Gross Hans Luder and wife lived after Luther's birth. Got some new and interesting slides. So far, finding where Luther's parents are buried has been a *dead end*!

The students here are fun, and they now have found a bicycle for me to use. David Ratke (PLTS Class of 1992 & 93, doctoral student in Regensburg) called; I will preach at his church in Regensburg December 15th.

It's going very well with the students, as they have not seen before a professor with a sense of humor, horrible German, and lectures without manuscripts. I'm having wonderful theological discussions with faculty, visiting former students, and also my dear German classmate from Hamma School of Theology at Wittenberg in Ohio, Willi Polster, who is now professor of Pastoral Care at Erlangen and who served as a CPE supervisor in Stanford and Berkeley for several summers.

My real struggle is to deal with all these theologians who are human chimneys and smoke all their waking hours! My asthma is not good.

Prof. Richard Riess and I will go to Coburg and Kronach (place of artist Lucas Cranach the Elder's childhood) this Friday and stop part way back at Erlangen for dinner in the home of Willi Polster.

The slides and life of Wilhelm Löhe have come to a standstill as I try to find these obscure places of his younger years, but I will have a nice presentation of slides and story eventually. I can tell that I ask questions here about Luther and Löhe which puzzle the faculty and students who just don't pay that much attention to either.

There is almost no mention of stewardship, so those lectures are received as if I just discovered a brand new idea no one ever thought of before!

I will soon visit the intern site of our alum Annemarie Czetsch south of Heidelberg. To do that I will take several trains and buses. My time here is rapidly coming to conclusion.

After Christmas I will travel to my ancestral village of Schmalenberg in the Rheinpfalz. I'll fly back to San Francisco and arrive on December 28th. Have a blessed Christmas.

July 17, 1999
Dear Friends and Family,

I'm back home and it's good to be here again, but the time spent in Germany was a wonderful, productive, and restful period for me. I'm grateful to the students, faculty, and administration of the Augustana Hochschule for making my stay so pleasant. I enjoyed very much good dialogue with many students. The accommodations were comfortable, the food in the mensa was delicious, and the conversations enriching.

I hope I contributed by preaching at Abendmahl (eucharist), lecturing each week, and counseling many students.

I was able to complete two small companion volumes which will be out in print in about one year. Working titles are: *The Miracles Of Jesus And Their Flip Side* and *The Parables Of Jesus And Their Flip Side.*

I'd like to tell you about the time spent with grandson, Jacob Schmalenberger, who arrived in Germany on June 18. We drove about four hours from Neuendettelsau to the Rhein/Pfalz and slept in the attic room of Pastor Moser of Schmalenberg. There are no rooms to rent in this little village.

Village sign and Jacob L. Schmalenberger

53

We had a nice afternoon with Gretel Schmalenberger-Feike and her family including "Uncle" August in nearby Heltersberg. She is slowly recovering from her accident, but still has double vision.

We met several more Schmalenbergers. One was a ten-year-old school boy and his grandfather, Walter. We also visited with our closest relative, Marta Schwab, who is descended from one of the brothers of my immigrant great-grandfather, Nicolaus. Nearby in Trippstadt, where there are quite a few Schmalenbergers, we visited Helmut Schmalenberger, a "Frischdienst," who sells produce and milk products in many little villages around.

The trip through the forest to the Hundsweiler-Sagemuehler (former sawmill) where our ancestors were born was interesting. There is a house built on the foundation of the old one which burned. The old people tell of our ancestors returning from worship in Schmalenberg, singing again the hymns as they walked home through the forest. You could hear them for miles!

When we climbed up in the church tower built in the fourteenth century, we noticed that the bells were much newer than the church building. The Burgermeister told us that the Nazis had taken the older bells and made ammunition out of them. This was a common practice throughout Germany.

Heinz Schober, the forester, took us wild boar hunting one night in the forest near the Hundsweiler, but we didn't get a shot at any.

On the return trip we stopped at Heidelberg to see Europe's oldest university and its famous castle.

Other places Jacob has seen are the famous WWII concentration camp, Dachau, Albrecht Durer's home, Rothenberg on the Romantic Road, the German National Museum in Nurnberg, the little ancient villages of Wolfsram-Ashenbach, Ansbach, and Weisendorf where the Lechner-Schmidts are pastors.

Jacob has played a lot of soccer with the Hochschule students. Grandpa was very proud. He also attended my lectures and I hope HE was proud. Jake went one night to the once-a-week student bar and drank apple juice. He got to like the drink "apfelschorle" which is a mixture of apple juice and sparkling mineral water. The students had a rock concert one day on campus which Jake attended (and Grandpa went along!).

During these three months at the Hochschule, I spent considerable time at our dear friends' home, Wilfried and Annette Lechner-Schmidt. They are the pastors who adopted the four Liberian children as a result of my last stay in Neuendettelsau. They have moved to the little town of Weisendorf near Erlangen where storks roost on their parsonage and church roofs! I took part in their son John's baptism and served as Godfather (Pate) to Carol who is named after Carol Schmalenberger who was there at her birth in Liberia in 1987. I also served as assisting minister in Wilfried's installation in the new congregation which loves these black children, unlike their former congregation. We'll find ways to keep in close contact with the Lechner-Schmidts.

The Lechner-Schmidt family

A former student took me to Berchesgaden to see Koenig See and hike around it. We also went through the salt mine and up to Hitler's Eagle's Nest retreat. Then after staying in a pension with French-speaking people, we toured the castle still owned by the Wittelsbach family (descendants of King Ludwig I and II, Otto, and others).

55

I got back to Neuendettelsau in time to celebrate Kirchweih which is an annual observance of the founding of the village church. Often it is set in the weekend observance of the saint for which the church is named. The Bamberg Bavarian band played in a tent which was filled with at least 500. We "Schunkeln" (all lock arms and sway back and forth on the benches) as an eighteen-wheeler tank truck full of beer parked outside and ran a hose into the bar.

Good-byes at the Hochschule were moving. Meals in many faculty homes, a wonderful farewell party in Nurnberg (at the flat of Katzi Grossmann, a close friend) and students coming to my room with little gifts all day before departure. I returned home with many candles, trinkets, and beautiful cards and notes. The Germans know well how to say good-bye. During my stay we had bonded in a close friendship similar to some in Sumatra.

I elected to stay home this summer since I want to enjoy my short stay before I leave for Hong Kong on August 30.

My retirement years are full of blessings and opportunities for discipleship for which I'm grateful.

Hong Kong Reports from Lutheran Theological Seminary on Tau Fong Shan

Report #1
9/9/99

Since I have a phone line in my tiny apartment and my laptop along, I'll send an update from time to time. My trip to Hong Kong from San Francisco was thirteen plus hours long. I'm still waking at 4 a.m. and struggle to stay awake after 8 p.m. Tonight may be different as we are expecting a typhoon! We will have high winds and rain but up here on the top of Tao Fong Shan mountain there will be no waves! It's a beautiful place meaning the "mountain of the logos winds."

My apartment is comfortable. I am now remembering some things from our last time here: don't look in the kitchen corners or drink the water! Everything is built small. There are 121 steps up to the dining hall and my teaching space. I share office space with

The Lutheran Theological Seminary in Hong Kong

two Swedish part-time faculty and live in the noisy student housing. The weather is very hot and very, very humid!

This seminary (Lutheran Theological Seminary of Hong Kong) of 26 faculty and 200 students was established in Shekow, Hubei, China in 1913. It was moved to HK in 1948 and moved up here in 1992 on donated land owned by the Norwegian Christian Mission to the Buddhists which is now a Christian retreat center. The eight-year-old facility is beginning to show signs of needing maintenance. It includes an administration and classroom building, dining hall, chapel, two dormitories, and flats for married students and faculty. It is built in the traditional Chinese style and must be one of the most beautiful in the Third World (or any world).

Hong Kong is more than a city, being an archipelago of some 235 rocks and islands upon a squat mountainous peninsula. Our mountain rises high above the New Territory city of Shatin which is connected by rail to HK Island. HK was first established by the narcotics trade. Piracy was the first basis of HK crime, together with smuggling, and for years was the local way of life. In 1841 the British flag was raised here. In 1997 HK returned to Chinese sovereignty with a population of 5.8 million.

My teaching load increases by the hour: Biblical Preaching, Discipling in the Church, and a seminar on Christian Education. In addition, I have several presentations in the Lutheran Church of HK, and preaching assignments in the seminary chapel. I will serve as advisor to two students writing their theses. Because of the heart attack of a professor they asked me to do the Christian Education. It's been a long time since I taught this subject at Heidelberg College and means I must get up to speed at once by making visits to parishes with an interpreter this semester in order to be prepared for a full course next semester.

My Batak student is not here yet because of red tape of the People's Republic of China. I am also very concerned about Indonesia. Sounds like a killing of each other again. I hope I can get in there and out before it gets worse. Ache in northern Sumatra is the place that is ready to explode. That's near the Medan airport, not far from the STT-HKBP seminary where I taught two years ago.

The mix of international students here will provide me much opportunity to learn about their religion and culture. They come from Cambodia, Korea, Germany, Sweden, Finland, Norway, Indonesia, India, Burma, China, Philippines, and Nepal (I ate with them tonight), Thailand, and some others I can't remember. While the majority of the faculty are Chinese, we also have four or five other countries represented.

The Division for Global Mission of ELCA supports two of the Faculty: Ted Zimmermann and John LeMond and two students from Nepal.

The way they treat the former president of the school, Andrew Hsiao, is beautiful! He and his wife continue to live on campus and he can teach as he wishes. He also eats with the faculty whenever he wishes.

My welcome here has been very heartening. Faculty and staff whom I knew previously were especially gracious. Several former students came out from HK to say "hello." When I landed at the airport President Lam met me and then had to go on to Beijing to explain what the role of the church will be in the future of Hong Kong. I will be very happy to see his return. His wife has gone all out to make my stay comfortable.

There is so much to tell, I am writing another report already, for this time at least. Besides, we are going through a #10 typhoon right now and I can't get out to do anything else! All Hong Kong and the New Territories are shut down but to this moment we still have power which continues to threaten to go off at any moment. My short wave radio says it's the worst storm in many years in Hong Kong and up here it seems to be even worse because of being on top of this mountain.

The eye of the typhoon is upon us and there is an eerie calm and a gentle rain. Soon comes the back side and more of nature's wrath. Several of my students had me come eat with them during this calm. The rice was OK but I fear the other was something I did not recognize! They were proud and I forced it down. The storm has done a lot of damage up on this mountain! My few windows are plastered with green leaves and debris blown against them so I can't see much. These buildings have been built to withstand such stress so I am not in any danger, although there has been some flooding in dorm rooms and other seminary buildings. During the height of the storm I e-mailed our daughter in Florida as hurricane Floyd was battering them. I am very concerned about the hundreds of illegals hiding up here in the jungle on this mountain of the Logos wind. We'll organize to see about their needs after the back-side of the typhoon passes over.

Now to calmer things. I get the news twice daily, once in early morning on ABC from the previous night in U.S. and once also on the BBC in the evening. I read the *South China Morning Post* each day in the library. It talks a lot about "triads" which commit a lot of the crime. They seem to be like our Mafia families.

Speaking of families, the students are divided into "families" and we meet monthly. Herr Muehlhaus and I have the following in ours: Indian Orthodox, two Korean, two Burmese, a Cambodian, a Chinese, and one from Nepal.

I have three advisees working on their Master's theses:

1. A Korean writing on learning implications in Christian education
2. A Nepali on the Christian family in Nepal
3. A Chinese on the Bible and church on homosexuality

It will be a lot of work, but also a chance for me to learn much. I will lecture the next two weeks in a class on pastoral ethics. My two courses are well attended but I've had two drop the course on preaching because it was too much work. Some things are the same the world over.

I eat with the students and rotate to the various tables of ten. We have fish twice a day and usually two other dishes and always rice. Sometimes there is a soup made from boiled bones which we drink right out of our individual bowl. The food is eaten with chop sticks — one set to retrieve food to the rice bowl and another to move the food from the bowl to the mouth. On the weekend I eat with international students' families or walk down the mountain to Shatin. In my apartment I must boil all my water and keep apples, breakfast food, and peanut butter on hand. Milk is about $4.00 a quart!

"Punkin" and Howard do translation for chapel

We have worship four days a week. If the language is Chinese, we wear earphones for the translation to English. If I preach, the Chinese wear the phones. We all sing in our own language. On Fridays we have an assembly. I will speak on Theological Education.

This mountain was first purchased by The Christian Mission to the Buddhists, a Norwegian group. The land for the seminary was donated by them. The mission is now a retreat center with a congregation of worshipping Chinese Christians. Others worship on Sunday evenings in English. My first week here I went to this Buddhist-style building for my Sunday worship and communion. I was very sad to see the complex in this condition, as three fires have been set there. The little group met in another building but no one came to lead the service and preach. So I spoke on the text of the day. The reason for the devastating fires seems to be either disgruntled employees or an effort to get these Christians off the mountain. Sounds to me like the former. The library/archives did not burn, thankfully.

My Batak from Sumatra, Deonal Sinaga, arrived and has begun his studies. We will prepare him to teach in the STT-HKBP seminary as he works on his Master's here. When things calm down a bit in Indonesia after this fall's elections, I'll make a trip there to do some continuing education for the Panditas (Batak preachers) and Bible Women and will also preach at their big ordination service. It will be a chance to meet with the four students supported through the St. John's, Antioch, CA, student fund. It will be wonderful to see them again. There is one more who desperately needs his yearly tuition paid, one of my best students when I taught there. He sent word with Sinaga of his need. Sinaga has not yet received his student visa. We have only twelve days left to get it or he will have to leave again.

There was a strange sight last Sunday when I took the train and then the underground down for a walk along the harbor. Perhaps twenty to thirty thousand young Filipina women were seated on the closed streets and sidewalks in small groups eating, drinking, and socializing. They gather this way each Sunday coming out of the homes where they work as domestics. I have seen this somewhere else; it might have been Buenos Aires. I bought one little group Coke and talked with them. Some of their stories were of abuse here. They had to be out of their homes all day on Sunday. Others were escaping a tough life in the Philippines. Two of the seven spoke OK English, so I am going to do that again, taking one of my Filipina students along.

I like what I am doing here. I have a deep sense of God's purpose and feel well liked and respected. To have this responsibility of preparing these students to go back to their home countries and effectively preach and teach the gospel is humbling. There are so many who could do it so much better than I, but what a wonderful learning experience for me! Sometimes the evenings are long and lonely but it is worth it. We'll try to open the school tomorrow. Here comes the backside of the typhoon with the wind's direction reversed!

Another typhoon is expected this next weekend, though not so strong as the last one. For my walk this morning I made my way through all the fallen trees to the cross which towers over Shatin. I shot a roll of film hoping to write some poetry about the way to the cross. I have written a verse to thank the Larssons (missionaries from Sweden who served in Tanzania and with whom I shared office space) and Mabel Wu (seminary music professor who has visited PLTS) for a meal the night before the typhoon:

Celebration of a typhoon
Before Tau Fong Shan's furious storm,
we dared the wind and challenged the rain
with food, drink, and precious fellowship.
Next early morning York proved its stuff.
We hunkered down in frightful reverence.
Cam came next as a sacred wet reminder.

Yesterday I moved into my own office; it will be a good place for my writing. It's air conditioned, has a computer (with instructions in Chinese!), and is in the middle of the Chinese faculty offices. This is probably a strategy of President Lam, as more and more I have become a fragile bridge between Chinese and International (students and faculty). The tension is even more obvious in the student body.

All is well here. Tonight is the moon festival for the Chinese. This morning's worship was meaningful with lots of lanterns used in place of candles. In the courtyard afterward we had mooncakes and fruit. I have enough mooncakes to last a month! Students have been bringing them to me all day. Lam, Tak Ho explained the reason for moon festival which did not make it clear to me at all. It has something to do with cultural myth.

I now have five doctoral students in practical theology in addition to my regular classes. What a challenging time I'm having. Former PLTS exchange student for one year, Solomon Wong, is here working on a Master of Divinity degree. I went to his neighborhood on Tuesday for the evening meal with his new wife. She is also a grad of this seminary and a pastor in a Methodist church. We then walked the streets of Mong Kok, a neighborhood in Hong Kong, along with one-half of the population of Hong Kong!

Seeing Deonal Sinaga from Sumatra wearing my clothes on campus is quite an emotional experience! They fit him very well and I don't think anyone knows where they came from. He is working with me in practical theology and will do a minor in New Testament with Ted Zimmermann. That should equip him well to return home and teach in the seminary in Pematang Siantar. His program and scholarship is for two years. Today he got another week's extension on his visa. We pray by then for his student visa to be granted.

I see nothing good ahead for Indonesia. I predict chaos and lots of bloodshed. The students will not be appeased, the military will not give up power, the government will not give up their corruption, and their nature has always been to love to fight.

I have run into a major problem with a couple of Korean women. Their husbands beat them. So I am trying to set up some marriage counseling in Korean language. This is very much a part of their culture. One is the wife of a pastor.

I continue to make progress on using this computer. I have now figured out Word for doing my documents and can run the spell check. Using it will help my spelling also. I was just able to check my Tau Fong Shan's seminary piece. Wow! I missed a bunch.

Our last international student arrived today from Hungary. I will have to see if she knows our former Hungarian exchange student at PLTS. She will be my fifth tutorial in practical theology. I will get them together Thursday evening to see if they can critique and help and learn from each other. This promises to be my most rewarding teaching. I got valuable experience in this method in Germany. They will have come from Burma, Korea, Nepal, Hong Kong, and Hungary.

When I preached this week in chapel, my narrative style surprised (astounded) many. I'll preach twice in October, once for Reformation. I will also show my "Life of Luther" slides to the

65

entire community. Next, the Swedish professor and I will do an All Saints communion service when I will preach again. Then there are the recordings to do for an English radio station for daily devotions. I am also scheduled to give a fifty-minute lecture on "Theological Education and Pastoral Formation" for the entire campus on the 8th. I just don't know how to make that subject of interest! It will take all my communication skills and a powerful Holy Spirit.

Now I'll walk with the Scandinavian students to Shatin for the lanterns along the river.

09/26/99

It's Sunday morning and a #8 typhoon warning has been hoisted. It should be here by noon so again we are all hunkered down waiting its vengeance. York was a #10 and took down many trees, stripped bark off some, broke out windows, and flooded first floor rooms. The radio just announced that airlines, buses, offices, ferries, trains, and underground are all closed. We don't have school when it's a #8, but by tomorrow it may be OK if we have power. This is something I did not know about to anticipate. My quarters are quite secure and I'll use the time to learn some basic words in Chinese. My neighbors from Nepal brought good bread and a kind of potato for supper which saved me from tea, toast and peanut butter. The news just now told us to stay indoors!

The ELCA's Asian studies group was through here last week. I ate and spent some time with them which I enjoyed very much. They all knew me and I knew a few of them (Agnes McClain and Bill Willms).

Deonal went to immigration to get an extension on his two-week visitor's visa and they would only give him one more week! Let's pray he gets the student one within that time. I'm not sure what he is to do if he does not. I'm trying to stay out of it. No word on mine yet either. Some of the problem may be that the last typhoon did a lot of damage to the immigration offices.

I have located a German restaurant way up the railroad. Wonderbar!!!

Triads are often mentioned in the *South China Morning Post*. They seem to be like our Mafia as the major source of crime and corruption. The other news is the arresting of many in China for doing exercises called "qi gong." It is connected to the Falun Gong sect. I'm interested and will find out more. Maybe Bethany will have to be careful! (Our daughter is coming to Hong Kong for a Wu Shu tournament.) We take our human rights so for granted.

My guidelines for getting into a culture are: 1) eat the food, 2) dance to the music, 3) read the poetry, 4) try to speak the language, and 5) learn the local history. I'm eating the food every day, a colleague is teaching me to dance, Esther Lam promises to get a famous poet translated for me (The Late Poems of Meng Chiao), I'm getting some basic words by constant hearing. Retired President Andrew Hsiao is a marvelous source of history as he was born in the seminary in China and was a first year student when they all had to come out of China in 1948. They arrived here in sixteen cars (about seventy people in all).

Nine percent of the population is Christian. Not counted are the illegals who hide up here in these mountains. They hang on under the trains as they come out of mainland. When the train stops at Shatin at the foot of Tau Fong Shan they run up into the jungle around the seminary. Getting hungry, they break into our place or rob people in the area. A couple weeks ago a student caught one fishing with a bamboo stick for his clothing right through his dorm window! I thought it was much more funny than the students did. When I tried to lay out some clothing for him to take, the students were very puzzled except for Deonal who had an understanding look on his face.

There is a heavy smog over Tau Fong Shan tonight from the smoke of Shatin, from the nearby valley where Buddhists cremate, and the secret campfires the illegals burn. The Logos wind will waft over us all and we will be cooled and able to breathe its promise. *Hiya!*

There is a mountain in the new territories of Hong Kong where years ago Norwegians began a ministry to reach out to Buddhist monks. At its beautiful heavily-wooded peak, on ground donated by the mission overlooking Shatin's high rise apartments, is located a theological seminary. The mountain is called Tau Fong Shan which means "the Mountain of the Logos Wind." The school is named the Lutheran Theological Seminary which means pastors and leaders for the church are prepared here.

It's a meaningful concept. The wind of God's word blowing over this holy hill is not missed by its faculty or students. In September '99 the wind of Typhoon York blew with much more force than those who named the mountain ever had in mind! We were all reminded of the awesome power of God whose word we proclaim. The seminary withstood the storm as it has had to do with many kinds of storms down through its 85 years of history.

A global family

There is a rich mix of cultures, nationalities, and languages over which the more genteel Logos winds blow today. The faculty is made up of 26 full- and part-time scholars coming from Sweden, Finland, America, Norway, Germany, Denmark, and Hong Kong. They instruct a student body of 200 even more diverse. The future of many congregations and seminaries in our global family is being shaped in this sacred seed bed of the prophets as the church's leadership is being formed.

There is a diversity of denominations as well. Pentecostal pastors climb the hill seeking further education. Methodists ascend to work on a second degree and a Roman Catholic priest rides the bus up the mountain to teach. All contribute to the meaningful variety which reflects the profile of God's world wide church.

It's not always easy living and studying together even with the Logos breeze to cool us. Daily worship in Ming Chieh chapel has to be conducted in several languages with headphones for those who need a translation. Because we are far less than perfect, some-times Chinese feel as though their school is being taken over by the students from Philippines, Burma, Finland, Taiwan, Sumatra, India, Nepal, Cambodia, Norway, Sweden, etc. On other days the many international students are resentful of so much Chinese language and culture. Both put a lot of energy into this year's theme, "loving each other," as they are convinced Christ would have them do it here and out in the real world of their parishes.

Faculty struggle valiantly to bring along their students who are not working in their primary tongue. These professors are well-educated and very determined to protect the academic integrity of the school. They work hard at realizing the dream of foremothers and forefathers of an international family preparing for effective discipleship. The missionaries add a special flavor of calling, dedication, and global perspective.

A good investment

Global mission organizations, individuals, and the Lutheran churches who financially support this school of the Logos winds can be confident they are making a good investment because of the solid teaching and effective preparation for ministry that takes place on this mountain.

A dynamic and compassionate president, Lam Tak Ho, academic dean Ted Zimmermann, and a board of nine trustees have a vision of what is possible and what's needed in the 21st century. They empower us to do our task at our full potential.

Those who can afford to contribute money in support of the Lutheran Theological Seminary can find very few reasons not to do so. As a retired U.S. seminary president who has lectured as an ELCA Global Mission Volunteer in Suriname, Argentina, Bavaria, Liberia, Jamaica, Sumatra, the U.S., and Hong Kong, I can witness first hand to the great value of this school of the prophets far up on Tau Fong Shan.

Words of praise are not enough either. My own checkbook will need to reflect my confidence and support as the Logos winds continue to blow even through it.

From Kathmandu to Yuen Long

Report #5: Sonam Goes to Church
(Written for The Lutheran magazine)

It's not an easy Sabbath to walk down our mountain, Tau Fong Shan, then ride the train to the New Territories town of Yuen Long to catch a bus to the center of town where there waits yet a smaller bus. Winding through the huge stacks of shipping containers, it turns onto a narrow dirt road running across low swampy land and eventually stops at the congregation's worship space. But Sonam Kabo, a student at Lutheran Theological Seminary in Hong Kong, feels a deep sense of call to be with his Nepalese brothers and sisters to shepherd, counsel, preach, worship, and fellowship with them.

Sonam, 38, and wife Rita, 35, both came with their two daughters, Keren and Priya, to study at the seminary in 1998. They plan to return to Nepal, a small country between India to the south and China to the north, to do Christian ministry where approximately 87% of the population is Hindu. They are excited about the growth of Christianity from about 30,000 in 1990 to 200,000 in 1998. Both come from Christian parents, with Rita's converting more recently.

On this Sunday morning he has brought with him two guests. Timothy Yoon, a Korean former classmate, will speak of his experience with Christians in Pakistan. One of Sonam's professors at LTS, ELCA Global Mission Volunteer Jerry Schmalenberger, will preach and teach these new Christians about discipleship. Rita, who is doing her Master's thesis on the Christian Family in Nepal, and her two children are elsewhere attending an Anglican Sunday School in nearby Shatin.

The worship space is donated by a Chinese couple who provided these immigrants from Nepal a place for their church. To get to the sanctuary the little congregation must pass through the house, built on sinking, crooked stilts and cobbled together from scavenged scraps of corrugated metal and black moldy lumber covered with tar paper. At the entrance near the pool of badly polluted stagnant water, little children with black hair, round eyes, and golden

The Nepali Worship building

brown skin greeted us with the traditional Nepalese greeting of palms together as praying hands and a humble lowering of the head.

The sanctuary itself is constructed out of scraps of lumber, sheets of plywood sealed with mailing tape, and corrugated metal. Electrical wiring was secured by bent-over nails. Even so, the little edifice held together on its pieces of granite and rock floor when the recent category 10 typhoon York blew across the New Territories. And when it rained hard during the service there were no leaks. The chancel was outlined by a blue cloth fastened by thumb tacks. A handmade varnished cross and pulpit made up the furnishings.

Women and girls on the left and men and boys on the right sat on red and black chairs so small that they brought me a larger one in fear I would fall off. Barefoot for inside and cleaned up for church, the casually dressed congregation began to sing. It sounded like a blend of African Kpelle and Sumatran Batak as a synthesizer, two guitars, rattle, and a tied-to-the-knees animal skin drum accompanied them. The women took turns keeping time by passing around a tambourine.

Two lay persons led the worship, mostly periods of simultaneous praying aloud, hymn singing, and reading scripture. This was what they knew so far which made up worship. In that unrestrained exuberance the spirit seemed so genuinely present.

71

Timothy told of miraculous things he had seen in his trip to Pakistan and I preached about Pentecost and the call to discipleship for all God's people. It felt as though this was all new to those who feasted on every word. Bread and wine were distributed, more praying, and the service was over. It hadn't been *Lutheran Book of Worship* liturgy. Far from it. But the important stuff was there: singing, praying, praising and thanking God, preaching of the word, reading of scripture, witnessing, and the real presence in communion. The liturgy could come later as they learn more about their new religion or feel the need for it.

And there was that infectious joy. A joy not the opposite of unhappy because these folks had plenty of reasons to be unhappy. They live hard lives. This was that distinctive Christian joy which is the opposite of unbelief.

It was to their young countryman Sonam they turned for guidance on how to do this new thing called Christian worship. A few words quietly said, a nod of approval from Sonam helped the leaders on. I wondered as he translated my sermon on discipleship who really knew best the subject.

With jelly sandwiches and Fanta, these pilgrims in a foreign land gathered outside for fellowship. They wouldn't see each other or speak their native tongue for another week and hung onto every precious moment of this time together. Now that they were Christians they had many questions to ask Sonam about how to live in this new land. One couple told of Hindu grandparents who put the traditional red mark on their offspring's forehead. Was it all right to leave it there? Other congregations would not allow them in church with such a mark. The answers were simple, biblical, and always reassuring.

These Nepalese spoke of their dream of having a church in town and getting out of this remote swampy area. They prayed Sonam and Rita one day could be their pastors. But since the ELCA and DSM (Danish Santel Mission) have granted a scholarship in order for them to work in Nepal, Sonam told them he must do just that and go back to Kathmandu to serve in that new Christian community even though Rita cannot yet be ordained in their Aradhana Church. They will keep their commitment.

But for now the youth choir had to practice and a problem had to be settled by an impromptu committee who discussed for a long time while seated on the dirt floor of the house. Sonam was there, and so they must seek the counsel of their theologian for the day. The advice was gentle and affirming.

At the house on crooked stilts where many families live, in the bus, upon leaving the two bus stops, and at each intersection as we walked through the town teeming with people, we said our goodbyes. And as we climbed the Mountain of the Logos Wind returning to the seminary I was certain that wind of the word had been with us and those Nepalese Christians as well.

Hong Kong Reports Continued

Report #6: Holidays, Seminary Life, and Visitors at Tau Fong Shan
10/17/1999

Today is a holiday called "Chung Yeung Festival" when the Chinese visit their ancestors. It's a little like our Memorial Day and has to do with a myth about a man who went hiking. When he returned to the village, all had been killed by a plague. So everyone hikes on this day, often to the graves of their ancestors. Tau Fong Shan is crawling with people hiking and visiting the graves, some scattered around the seminary. Every once in a while I hear firecrackers which are the traditional way of celebration. The little Christian cemetery has had many visitors also. Yesterday I gathered stories there about when, and how, they became Christians. Since each stone has a picture of the deceased on it, I find the place inspirational. (See "Tau Fang Shan's Daughter" in my booklet, *In Celebration.*)

Yesterday my Batak student, one from Norway, and I went up to Sheung Shui on the train to re-enter the country. So I am now officially in Hong Kong on a work visa. But they gave Deonal just two more weeks on his visitor's visa, again. We have some hope that next Thursday he will get the student visa when he and the dean will go to the Office of Immigration on a motorcycle.

The suicide of one of our young missionaries to China from Arlington Heights, Illinois, has us all in shock. Twenty-five years old and single, he came out here in August as a teacher (as you must do in China). He was not happy with his circumstances last month, but there were no clues as to his state of mind. He used a hose, plastic bag, and gas. They are making heroic efforts to get embalming and transportation arranged as he requested in a note. However, cremation there may be the only solution. I am curious as to what testing and orientation is done on these two-year people before they come over.

John and Carol Jarrett were here last week. They have been dear friends of ours ever since I was their pastor in Tiffin, Ohio, in the '60s. Going after them to the Marriott in Hong Kong, by train and then the underground, made the contrast between it and Tau Fong Shan where I live very obvious. They got to meet many of my students from many different cultures. We ate lunch in the seminary dining hall which was quite a contrast with the wonderful steak and beer dinner to which they treated me later that evening. One of the joys of our lives right now are the friends from our many years of ministry, just like many of you who receive these reports and so many who have responded by e-mail.

Just a few things about our student life. We worship each morning at 10 a.m. with a faculty member leading the worship, wearing headphones for a translation. Students also conduct their own services each evening before dinner, but on Sunday all go to a regular church usually in their own language. Students cannot leave campus without permission and the gate to the dorm is locked at 11 p.m. All must attend a special assembly every Friday where a lecture is given (even the Master's students must be there). We are divided into "families" of about eight which meet one Friday a month much like our growth groups at PLTS. Unlike the U.S., a professor must grant permission ahead of time for an absence from class and assignments are always ready with extra work, not required, often also done!!

By the way, every Saturday and Sunday there are weddings in our Ming Chieh chapel. This is because most of the little Lutheran congregations meet in a flat and thus have no church building or parking for such a crowd. So they come to this beautiful mountain of the Logos wind.

Susan Giantvalley asked about transportation and food. There are several cars here. Although they don't like to, taxis come up and down the mountain for a price. And the seminary has a little diesel bus (like PLTS) which goes up and down to the train station. From there you can go anywhere. The students and I most often walk down to the train in Tai Wai and then we wait until several gather at the taxi stand to share the cost of returning. Meals are provided with the exception of Saturdays and Sundays. We sit ten at a round table. The menu is very predictable: always a whole fish (head included), one bowl of rice, a dish of a vegetable, and one of a meat. We reach with shared long chop sticks to retrieve the food to our bowl of rice and then use our own chop sticks to put it in our mouths. It is quite acceptable to drink from the bowl, as it is to put the bowl to your mouth and scoop the food in (a maneuver I have not yet mastered, but the students love to see me try — with the results being rice all down the front of me and resting finally on that shelf my belly provides when I sit now). I buy Nissan dried soup, crackers, and peanut butter for the weekends.

One of our first congregations on this mountain celebrated its 45th anniversary yesterday and its founder was here for a visit last week. Many of our missionaries have belonged there. Notice that China just celebrated its fiftieth year of communism. So five years after that upheaval, the church got going here with many forced to come out of China.

During the years of my ministry, mission strategy has changed. We have moved from dependence to independence, now on to a time of interdependence and accompaniment. We see our churches around the world as our partners in mission at least equal with us and most often better equipped to do the work in their own culture. We missionaries support the indigenous leaders in their leadership. Grace Lutheran Church in Tsuen Wan sends missionaries to Bavaria and to Taiwan.

Compared with my last visit here, I believe I can tell some of the differences since the take-over by China. Student and work visas are harder to obtain. They tore down a Taiwanese flag flown in front of a store. People are arrested for doing an exercise connected to the Falun Gong sect. Those who criticize the government are forbidden to travel to events in China. And China continues to bankrupt itself by single-mindedly trying to be self-sufficient in its food supply. They often refuse to import where, in our global economy, it would be much cheaper. So reports are falsified and Chinese people are starving. Then there is this incessant pursuit of the illegals from China who come to Hong Kong. Most mornings now the police set up here near my dorm room in plain clothes watching for them. When they catch one it is a brutal arrest.

Every so often there comes a teaching moment that is so wonderful it's hard to keep my feet on the ground walking out afterwards! In the class on "Discipling in the Parish" I was going to lecture on the symbol of the steward. I had asked each student to look at about ten passages in the Bible and be ready to discuss them in class. As an afterthought I added that they should also research what words and metaphors were used for steward in their own languages and culture. The results were spectacular and we all learned so much! I will not forget those students going to the board, writing in their own language, explaining the various uses of the words and how they thought it added to our understanding of the concept. I will share with you and the stewardship newsletter of LLM the richness of what I learned that day from students of India, Cambodia, Hong Kong, Nepal, Sumatra, Myanmar (Burma), Philippines, and Korea. I'll use that teaching technique much more now that I have stumbled upon it.

My teaching of homiletics is fun, too. I had to come up with a way of critique that would not cause "loss of face." Written sheets and private sessions work but I do regret the loss of all benefiting from common open critiquing. If I can arrange video taping and then individual sessions it will also help.

To my German friends who receive this: I did attend a Chinese Octoberfest in a hotel on the island with several faculty members and hoisted one (or two) in your honor. It was not quite like Franconia or little Neuendettelsau!!

Our daughter Bethany Allison, a fourth grade teacher, visits soon. In January I hope to have a group of PLTS students with me upon my return for their cross-culture requirement. The ELCA Division for Global Mission Program Director for Asia, Pastor Thomas F. Schaeffer, will be here to visit with us missionaries on November 7. Thanksgiving will be with a group of St. Olaf students.

Each morning I am greeted anew by a frog in a catch basin and a bird in a black barked tree as I climb the 121 steps to the dining hall. It is as if God welcomes me to this mountain:

Intimate Presence

Just above the Reichelt round moon gate,
up the steps to holy Ming Chieh chapel
in a voice which reverberates deep passion,
calls out a Chinese frog for companionship
from a gray concrete accidental cistern.
A songbird in the tree ridicules the verbosity;
But we know the joy of intimate presence.

There is a large concrete cross on this mountain which was erected years ago and towers over the city of Shatin. The former Norwegian Christian Mission to the Buddhist monks built it here. The interesting thing is that many Chinese who live in Shatin place mirrors in their windows to reflect its powers and protect them from it. Would that we Christians took the power of the cross as seriously! Or tried to reflect its power for others.

It is cooler at last. Right now the temperature is 28c with the humidity at a usual eighty percent. Another statistic: unemployment in Hong Kong is at 6.2%.

Our Sumatran student does not yet have his student visa and got two more weeks on his visitor's. I went into China on the train last Saturday and came back with my work visa so am now legally here and legally working. Looks like I'll have a few PLTS students coming back with me after Christmas to do their required cross-culture experience. One will be Kelly Leichsenring from St. John's, Des Moines, where I was her pastor when she was a little girl. She is very dear to Carol and me. Bethany Allison, our daughter, visits for a week next week.

I now know the courses I will teach next semester: Teaching Luther's Catechism, Homiletics 3 (which is Preaching the Occasional Services), and Parish Administration (in Chinese and English) and will continue the individual tutorials as well. For Lutheran and Methodist pastors, I am scheduled to do a major continuing education series on preaching over a four-week period on HK Island. They are expecting a very large crowd for that. So far the preaching I have heard here is mostly lecture delivered in a scolding manner.

I had one of my most interesting classes (at least for me) in Discipling last week. I handed my piece to them on "The Stewardship of the Family" the week previous and told them to prepare how this related to their own family. One after one they told of the pain of being the first or second generation Christian in the home and how that put them outside the family traditions and events.

79

Tears came as they told of what a disappointment they were to their parents. Such things as getting married, having babies, holidays based in Buddhist religion, and living in tiny apartments with several generations wanting to practice their religious customs including the use of josh sticks, the burning of incense, the placement of the Buddhist altar, votive light, and offering of fruit. One agonized that she had no model of how to raise her children as Christians.

One married woman, who is the first one in her family to become a Christian and must live with her old Buddhist father-in-law, was forced to decide what to do last week when we had the national Chung Yeung holiday, the time they all go out to the graves of their ancestors. He asked her to help him to prepare the necessary foods for the offering. She did not want to do it as a Christian but felt she should help her old father-in-law. Privately, I advised her that St. Paul faced a similar problem with food offered to idols. I told her to help the old man to carry out his customs including getting him to the graves and simply explain it to God in her prayers that night. God would understand and might even enjoy the variety. And just maybe it was the same God with a different name and way of approaching a different people anyway! This blatant heresy seemed helpful to her and her pastor-husband who didn't know what to do from his rather fundamentalist theology.

Students told of the abusive fathers and the male chauvinism in their homes and countries. They spoke of beatings of themselves and their mothers and of the low regard of female babies. It ran through all the reports of Cambodia, Myanmar, Sumatra, India, Nepal, Korea, Taiwan, and China.

When Swedish Missionary Dr. Birgitta Larsson lectured on feminist theology at the seminary assembly last Friday, all the Korean students and Chinese faculty stayed away. I'll ask for a discussion of this at our faculty meeting next Friday. She speaks the truth in such a gentle and persuasive way. She began her presentation with a prayer from *Children's Letters to God*: "Dear God, are boys better than girls? I know you are one, but try to be fair." — Silvia.

I had lunch at the home of former president of LTS Andrew Hsiao last week with eighty-year-old David Vickner. He is the former head of the Board of Foreign Missions of the ULCA. Born in China, he was a missionary there also. The three of us and his new wife talked far into the afternoon. Here were a couple saints of the church.

Speaking of saints, I'll preach next Friday on the All Saints theme. In this culture they think of saints as dead people who were "good" when they were alive. I will try to open up the concept of living saints, sanctification, priesthood of all, communion of saints, and Paul's teaching and writing on a "holy" people, etc. I also preach on Thursday and will do a Reformation theme and talk a bit about the recent agreement with the Roman Catholics. It will be very new to many here. On Wednesday I'll show my slides on the life of Luther to the entire seminary community. They know little of Luther. If I keep moving around the world, I probably can use that slide show a few more times!

I have learned from my students about the culture and religion of Myanmar which used to be called Burma. (Burmese is one of many ethnic groups and the name of the language the educated speak.) Those who favor democracy still try to call the country Burma. LTS has agreed to help them upgrade their seminary faculty so we have four here. The practice of Christianity is not easy there. It is impossible to get a permit to build a church and they must have a permit to have a Christian celebration as well. The population is about 90% Buddhist with a military dictatorship which does not want education for its people because the educated might cause discontent. The schools and universities have been closed for more than three years. The only way students can come here is as tourists and then try for a student visa from Hong Kong (which is not easy either). In classes Henry, Stella, "Mr. Burma," and "St. Pau" all speak different dialects because each comes from a different tribe. They wear western clothes and do not suffer at all from the heat or humidity as they move very slowly from place to place. Around the dorm they wear their more traditional skirt tied in front called a "longy."

81

I now have six individual tutorials. They meet all together in addition to our individual sessions. The every-three-week-together learning group sessions are very rewarding as they report on their research:

Hungarian — on the pastor as caregiver — Dorottya Naggy
Nepali — on the Nepali Christian family — Rita Kabo
Indonesian Chinese — on pastoral care of the homosexual —
    Lam Chiu Fai (Peter Lam)
Batak — on how to teach practical theology — Deonal Sinaga
Korean — on how various age groups learn — Nisa Han
Myanmar — on pastor as counselor — Thang Suan Pau

It's really beginning to work as they check up on each other, offer critique, suggest books and new approaches, and learn about the other's subject. Of course, I'm the one who really learns. I have never worked so hard academically nor enjoyed it so much.

I have a story in the November issue of *The Lutheran* called "Lutherans and Their Tea" about my trip last year to Argentina and Uruguay. Here is another story I wrote recently for publication in *Lutheran Women Today*. You might give it to your pastor. It will preach.

Man Suk Yee Preaches on Strong Legs

I had just finished a tutorial with Thang Suan Pau, one of the professors of the Myanmar (former Burma) seminary, as our pledge to help upgrade their faculty. It was now a few minutes before time for worship. I was looking forward to some quiet time in our Ming Chien chapel. As I arrived at the door one of my students in Discipling, Man Suk Yee, the only Christian in her family, came to me to say she was to give her senior sermon today and was so glad I came!

Suk Yee then told me her legs were shaking and she was afraid they would "let down" while she was preaching. Tears welling in her beautiful eyes she asked what to do? I told her I would go forward with her, sit close and pray for her to have strong legs. While she preached, I prayed my first prayer for a woman's legs with my eyes open watching hers. They stopped their nervous shaking and became stronger and stronger as she preached with a more

Man, Suk Yee

and more powerful voice. Five minutes into the sermon she could have played fullback for the Oakland Raiders.

After the sermon, I offered a prayer for preachers everywhere that they might be *strengthened* in their proclamation. After the service Suk Yee politely shook my hand and bowed thanking me for the support as tiny Chinese tears of joy and relief ran down her golden cheeks. The Dean came up and told her how much stronger her delivery was this day. With a twinkle in her eyes she told him it was "... all in the legs." He looked bewildered. But I understood. I never told a person, but at supper that night several students called me a new Chinese name they had never used before, "keng chong ga ka." It means "old strong legs"! "Therefore, strengthen your feeble arms and weak knees" (Hebrews 12:12).

Last Saturday this computer crashed and I could not get it started again. The Norwegian Old Testament Professor, Terje Stordalen, worked on it and finally got it going. Now all the directions are in Norwegian. Words like *arkiv, rediger, innhold, elikett,* and *spesilt* appear. My hearing aid stopped on the same day but I was afraid to ask him to fix it!!

In addition to Mickey Mouse coming to Hong Kong, so is the Weimar edition of Luther's works. We faculty want so much to get an Asian Luther study institute established here. By next year we hope to have raised the necessary funds to launch such a resource for all of Asia. We are hoping we might at least find enough to bring a couple Luther scholars to LTS to hold a celebration of the collection's arrival. I feel some obligation to keep Luther and Lutheran before Christians here.

One of the living saints at LTS is Andrew Hsiao. Former president who came out of China with the seminary, he told me of those early days when they nearly starved, hunting frogs for their only food. They stole some salt to season them during cooking, but discovered there had been sand put in the salt to make it seem there was more of it. That day they ate frogs seasoned with sand and a little salt. How's that for salt of the earth?

The news keeps reporting that robberies and "criminal damage" are up 18 to 31%. The poor economy causes debt collection which is very violent.

The Rev. Tom Schaeffer met with us ELCA missionaries last Sunday night. There are three couples, an intern from Chicago's LSTC, and me. Tom is one of several program directors of the DGM. I was looking forward to his coming to Tau Fong Shan and talking over what we are doing in our ministries. He had us all come to his hotel, eat a dinner, and said thanks for all we do ... and we all went home.

I have worked with the D.Min. students this week. One is a dean of a three-self government-sanctioned seminary in the mainland, another is the Bishop in Taiwan. Others are from the Hong

Kong area. I learned so much. They are organizing a lecture tour they want me to do especially in China and Taiwan and Indonesia. Then back here for a while to continue work with them (two to three weeks each). Hay-chun Maak has written two major facts about China which I believe are correct: 1) It represents one of the largest unreached groups and, 2) It may become one of the greatest missionary *sending* nations! The Chinese population is 1.4 billion on the mainland and outside mainland is 50 million. There are about 7,000 Chinese churches outside China with 1,300 in the U.S. and Canada, 1,200 in Hong Kong, 2,500 in Taiwan and about 1,500 in SE Asia. What an opportunity! If I were just younger!

For Halloween the cook got a pumpkin for me. One of my students and I made a pumpkin face for outside my door (she is now called punkin). While carving it in the kitchen we caused quite a stir and a large group gathered to watch us. One committee meeting adjourned to see how we did it.

Our daughter Bethany was such a joy to have here last week. We went by public transportation to an ancient walled city up by the border, rode on a Chinese junk in Aberdeen harbor among all the boat people, climbed to the top of Victoria peak for pictures, climbed to the temple of 10,000 Buddhas, and went way out to the end of the line to see the three in one religion temple institute. The latter is an attempt to put together the Confucian, Buddhist, and Taoist religions. She also visited her Wu Shu tournaments on HK island. My students loved having her here in Chapel, one of my classes, and worship in Tau Fong Shan's church at the pilgrim's mass. My six students from PLTS coming over in January will do all this and much more for their cross-culture credit.

One of the things we saw on the way back from the walled village was a large and very old banyon tree in a little village. The tree was full of red and gold paper. These had been hung on the tree as prayers for blessings and good luck (something very important to Chinese). The tree is revered because of its age. After hanging there for a certain length of time the paper is burned, I think.

While we have the missionaries Peterson here now doing ministries among the thousands of Filipina domestic workers, I had no idea there were 20,000 Indonesians here doing the same thing. My

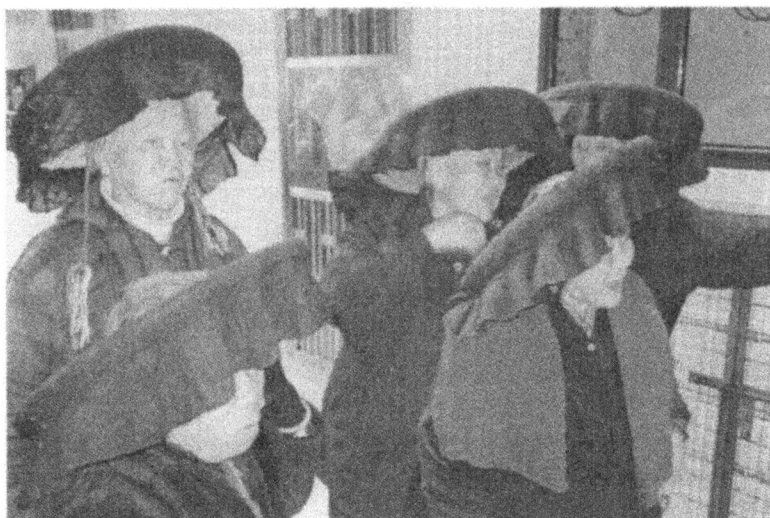

Hakka women at Walled Village outside Yuen Long, New Territories

Batak student was able to arrange a visit of seven of them. Through him I could talk with them in depth. They loved my use of the words I know in Indonesian and Batak. We will do an Indonesian fellowship in their embassy in a couple weeks.

It looks as though there might be a loosening up on the Protestant Church in communist Vietnam. If so, some little seminaries might be able to re-open. Since the withdrawal of U.S. troops 25 years ago the 25,000 members has increased to one million. The problem is that the only leaders were trained before 1975. If the Protestants are recognized like the Catholics and Buddhist we must be ready to step in and help with strengthening of the religious infrastructure. It seems as though we grow best when under persecution. And sometimes I think the best theological education happens in the least organized situations when an experienced pastor teaches an inexperienced one what to be and how to do it.

In my Discipling class I have learned of the Korean ways of sustaining their families by two ethical principles: the first is "heo" which means respect for old age. The second is "jaae" which is love and care of the young.

87

In my homiletics class Tshering "Rita" Kabo brought me to tears when she told in her practice sermon of how almost all the people in Nepal are Hindu. It is against the law to evangelize. One neighbor boy converted to Christianity and his Hindu father tried to kill him because of the disgrace he felt in the community. The father would have succeeded but for her intervention.

This week I have had so many responsibilities there has been no time for writing poetry or doing any work on my book manuscript. I was feeling sorry for myself as I held another tutorial with a student who is preparing to return to his Myanmar to teach in their new seminary. He has made such progress! *That* is my poetry for this week.

I preach this Sunday in Yuen Long in the congregation of new Nepali Christians again. It will be basic stuff like Paul had to do on his missionary journeys.

From the mountain of poisonous green bamboo snakes and large porcupines.

Impromptu Global Dancing (these will preach)

It was an extemporaneous happening there on the jungle-en-croached clearing in back of our little seminary up on Tao Fong Shan mountain. Because there is no food available on Saturday nights, some of our international students decided to pool what little they had. (We have done it before taking seriously the loaves and fishes of Galilee and it almost always works.)

A fire was built out of dead sticks available as a result of the recent typhoon. Over the fire was placed an old discarded wok filled with the inventory from our rooms. Milanie Catolico, a beautiful young woman from the Philippines, put chicken wings on a coat hanger and roasted them for everyone. (The Chinese must raise many-winged chickens, as that's the only part I ever see.)

Deonal Sinaga from Sumatra, a Batak with swarthy skin and black eyes which blended with the darkness, played his guitar. Soon we were all singing Batak songs he taught us. I have heard them before and I recognized the plaintive wail of missing one's *Bona ni Pinasa*. (That's the village of origin so important to Sumatrans.)

We all began to revel in the bond of our togetherness so far from home there on that little clearing in the snake and porcupine-inhabited jungle over which the Logos wind still blows. (Tau Fong Shan means the mountain of the Logos wind.)

The two young daughters of Sonam and Rita Tshering Kabo from Nepal began to dance playfully in the light of the fire. Yi, Narith, a slender muscular young man of light grey-brown complexion and one of the first Christians in Cambodia, encouraged the little performers. Chim Pich, president of the student association also from Cambodia, added affirmation in his own language. (They both are preparing to teach in that predominately Buddhist country.)

Then in the delightfulness of that moment Sonal Christian, a lovely Indian woman, got up and began to do her lively native dance, skipping in a circle and clapping her hands. Stella Min from Myanmar and Dorottya Naggy of Hungary started to follow.

89

Next came our usually reserved Orthodox Indian priest, Rajan George Nirayannoor. Soon the contagious dance had welcomed us all into the ever widening circle which now challenged the limits of the fire's illumination. (It is a graceful whirling, clapping, and skipping motion easily learned but a bit physical for the professor!)

Several Chinese watched in bewilderment from the top of the little hill. One new student from Malaysia wasn't sure Christians should dance at all. The security person, Thang Suan Pau, a Burmese with a powerful flashlight, scurried to see what the commotion was all about and soon joined in. And at lunch today there were whispers about people dancing behind the dorm ... even a professor ... and in bare feet! There were also knowing glances from eyes which seemed to sparkle more than usual. It was a global dance of God's own people. (Perhaps God's toe tapped as well that night because we were together and celebrating our bond of disciple love for each other.)

Return to Yuen Long

I traveled up to Yuen Long again last Sunday and preached and dedicated their new place for worship. They now meet on the second floor of a retail building in the center of Yuen Long in the shadow of mainland China. They met me with embarrassing bows with palms together as though praying.

At just the right moment the little congregation of Nepalese asked me to raise a blind on the window overlooking the teaming New Territory's village of Yuen Long. It said on the window: "Every Body Well Come to New Place, unc. H. K."

Sonam Kabo, a student in my Discipling class at the Lutheran Theological Seminary on Tau Fong Shan, had led the worship up until then, mostly spirited Nepali songs accompanied by men on guitars, drum, rattle, and an old synthesizer which drifted in and out of working. But the infectious clapping and tapping of the tambourine kept us dancing a bit as we sang.

After the blind was raised we prayed and prayed out loud — very loud and all at once. No doubt about it, the little group of about 55 were glad to be in their new worship space. Then as if by

90

Sonam Kabo and JLS during a children's sermon
in Nepali Church, Yuen Long, SAR

some unseen signal it was time for my sermon. Sonam, whose petition to have one more year on his ELCA scholarship has just
been denied, interpreted as I preached on the miracle of Jesus healing the man let down through the roof at Capernaum. I asked them
to expect healings and miracles in this place of worship too. It will
happen, too. For these new Christians take the preacher's word
literally and for exact fact. I had to tell them they need not make a
hole in the roof for such healings! After the two-hour service, an
elder presented me with a framed picture of the Annapurna mountain range of Nepal. We then moved the tiny stools around to make
way for the feast of Big Macs and clean water from across the
street.

Sonam sat next to me as a couple elders asked questions about
being a real church. What decides the gospel for the day? Where
do we find the name of the Sunday? How much should we put in
the sack (offering)? More and more gathered around, scooting those
stools in closer and closer until there were at least fifteen ques-
tioning and soaking up the hopefully unencumbered-by-culture

answers. "If God made Adam out of mud and Eve out of Adam's rib, does woman have any of God's mud in her?" This marvelous epiphany went on for an hour and a half. It seemed like a couple minutes. I was exhausted. We prayed out loud again and this time I did my best in English. I can do it too!

On the long train ride back to the seminary I began to think about what is essential for worship and what is just human tradition. Soon we have to ask what is essential for it to be Lutheran. Or need it ever be so? And what a difference a gift of $500 from a seminary classmate's widow and her husband from America had made for a little group of new Christians so far from home. We are global, indeed.

Only God knows what will happen next there in the second floor sanctuary across from a McDonald's which serves egg rolls and green tea. But for a while, at least, God's family will meet to hear the simple Gospel and the feast of God's presence will take place. And miracles and healings, too.

Table talks take on life of their own

Breakfasts at this seminary consist of each student preparing his or her own from a not very clean table on which is placed a can of dry rolled oats, Ovaltine, powdered milk, a jar of peanut butter (thank God), and one of U.S. rejected jelly. Nearby is a little 220-volt toaster and sack of semi-fresh bread. One tablespoon is used to do all the smearing. There is always piping hot water in the Chinese-clean kitchen.

Henry, the Dean of Studies in his seminary in Myanmar (Burma), always eats four pieces of toast during our table talk. We then gather around a table which will seat ten at 8:15 each morning to eat together and discuss theology until 9:10. I used to have a question ready to start the conversation but now they come well prepared. "Will the Egyptian pilot have a chance at salvation?" asks Yi from Cambodia. "Whose time was it to go?" says Milanie from the Philippines. "Punkin" from Hong Kong wants to know about "real presence" as she uses chop sticks on noodles. Sarah Joy from north India keeps promising to be there but can't get ready

My breakfast table talk (left to right): Mr. Win (Burma), Eddie (Hong Kong), Dorottya (Transvania and Budapest), Chim Pitch (Cambodia), Deonal Sinaga (Sumatra), Henry (Mynamar, Burma), and myself.

on time and the group isn't very welcoming to those who arrive late. The discussions always include "St. Pau," also from Myanmar, who understands little in English but who smiles a broad smile as if just being there will somehow instruct him.

Sinaga, my spiritual son, is always by my side where the rest insist he be, wearing my outgrown clothing. In typical Batak fashion he sometimes eats with his fingers. Along with Dorottya from Budapest, whose pastor was one of my PLTS students, Sinaga is developing into our finest theologian. He was elected by the student body to the cabinet and sits in on the faculty meetings representing the students.

When Henry finishes his fourth piece of toast covered with peanut butter and jelly, we know it's time for class and off we go to what *others* think is the first-learned theology of the day. We don't meet on Saturdays or Sundays and I really miss them as I eat corn flakes in my room.

Report #10: An Indonesian Advent on Hong Kong Island
11/28/1999

On the first Sunday in Advent with my Batak spiritual son by
my side, we took one train and three undergrounds jammed full of
women from the Philippines to the Indonesian Consulate on Hong
Kong Island in search of other Batak people and worship. I thought
it would put Sinaga from Sumatra, who studies with me here at the
Lutheran Theological Seminary on Tau Fong Shan, in touch with a
community which felt like his kinfolk.

The thousands of Filipinas were on their way to their weekly
reunions of Hong Kong domestics near Admiralty and Central stops
on the MTR. Short and courteous with black hair and rounder eyes
and dressed in western jeans, they poured out of the rail cars by the
thousands where their kinswomen anxiously greeted arrival in shrill
Tagalog language.

The Indonesian consulate is a large stone building amidst the
double-decker trams, shops, sidewalk hawkers, thousands of rush-
ing people with cell phones to their ears, and taxies — all of which is
Hong Kong. The MTR stop is Causeway Bay. It is loud, congested,
and very, very piquantly pungent. Here there are some Indonesian
restaurants and specialty shops integrated into the hodgepodge high
rise architecture. Neon signs compress and overhang the air space.

Many vacated shoes and a white-scarfed Muslim woman indi-
cated Islam on the first floor. Christians are up one and you can
leave on the shoes! Mostly vibrant young women from the many
islands of Indonesia made up the second floor Christians. While
they are paid less as domestics than the others because they do not
speak English (Chinese want their children to speak English), many
do immigrate here for the dependable, yet lonely and sometimes
oppressive, work.

The same worship area is used by Muslims on Friday and Roman Catholics in the evening, making the present fuss in Nazareth,
Palestine, seem inconsequent.

An elder led the approximately 350 golden brown with a hint of
gray complexioned worshippers, dressed western style, as they sang
and prayed in the spacious ballroom-like chamber. The Indonesian

words for the hymns were projected on a screen badly torn and laced at the top. Rhythmic clapping moved the singing along in a captivating way. For Sinaga it was like returning home; but not quite, as this was not Batak, although close. He and I sang and clapped with nostalgia to the synthesizer accompaniment enhanced by three women at microphones. Some raised their hands and gently swayed. My old Lutheran hands just don't want to do it. But sometimes I do sway just a little and even risk a toe tapping.

The praying is different from the Nepali or Korean loud, almost shouting, cacophony. This is a low feminine murmur-whine which seems like private crying, polite and respectful, and transports from the Indonesian soul to the heart of God. It always moves me deeply.

The pastor, Pdt. Arys H. Illu from Ambon near East Timor, who could pass for an African-American, was dressed in brown suit and tie, preached well using change of pace, narrative, and good homiletical style. His prayer was very close to the ground and politically specific. So much so that Sinaga, always humble and courteous, did not translate all of it into my eager ear.

We then did that which so often brings home close and unites us around the world. We prayed the Lord's Prayer and said the Apostles' Creed. After the thirteenth hymn and a blessing, the one and one half hour service was over. We were deluged with beaming welcomers with sparkling black eyes partly because "the long white one from America" sang in Indonesian but mainly because Deonal was an infrequent, young, single, and handsome Indonesian.

After promising to return and preach, we were escorted to a nineteenth floor private flat restaurant just for Indonesians named Setia Jaya and owned by our hostess, Tan Bie Kin. With our right hand fingers (left is for toilet only) we ate chicken satay and peanut sauce, beef in a hot spice, green stalks, and rice. The drink was green tea (I had hoped for Bintang beer). In the next room a birthday was being celebrated by Muslims singing their music. The tears in my eyes may have been over memory of my many precious friends in Sumatra or could have been the hot (like sac-sang) spice over the beef. In either case it was a great first Sunday in Advent filled with hope and anticipation.

95

Report #11: Student Quotations and Culture
12/05/1999

I have taught a course this semester with the requirement for a term paper at the semester's end. While reading these papers today, it occurred to me that some of these student comments would be interesting to those of you who receive these reports. The topic was *My Discipling Ministry*. I quote them exactly as they were written and spelled — not in their first language.

"And my grand mother was real inspirer who spend her whole life in a ministry through going to places in a boat to the villages on the bank of the great south Indian river Godavari."
— Geddada Sarah Joy, India

"I found out how exclusive and conservative I have become. It was always the 'theology of glory' that was emphasized and not the 'theology of the cross' and ... the most effective way to win a person to Christ and to make disciples is to live a life of word-deed consistency."
— Milanie S. Catolico, Philippines

"I think that Lutheran denominations are lack of mission than other denominations. I don't know why ... I am a born Christian. My mother is a sincere believer but not my father ... Disciple is a student who learn the worlds, actions and life style of his/her teacher in preparation to teach others."
— Daniel Jeong, Korea

"Almost my entire adulthood facing only killings and hatred since 1975 to 1989. The communist ideology-atheism is still influenced and widely practiced ... and Christians understood as human flesh eaters ... I went with my elder sisters who spoke to me about Jesus Christ. She was one of the first Christians in Cambodia."
— Yi, Narith, Cambodia.

"I was baptized from the Pastor in autum, he sprinkel water three times on my head. My tears come down from my eyes. I felt something special."
— Han Kum Ju, Korea.

"In my language (Myanmar) to be a steward means to be a treasure (Banda Soe) ... the one who keeps vauable things for others."
— Stella Min, Myanmar

"I've given materials to my husband as well as in-laws's family but the response is like, OK Jesus is another deity that I can go to ask for a blessing. So they will come once in a while to a church and go to the Buddhist temple at the same time."
— Park Kwang OK, Korea

"We have opened our home for terminated domestic helpers who may need a temporary shelter while looking for another employer."
— Rodrigo Felomino, Jr., Philippines

"But for Cambodia, steward meant 'chief of royal palace' and also meant as 'servant.' I love the word steward mean as a servant and as the one who bringing blessing to other, care for other in family and in the society ... We provide many toilets for the poor family who are living in the village ... My church does answer to some of these needs. We have school for poor children. We help the poor, given them sleeping net so that when they can escape from biting by mosquito, they can escape from many diseases ... As we break bread and drinking wine is in remember of Christ who died for us and as we are in His body. Therefore let us love one another because we share in the same bread and drink in the same cup of wine."
— Chim Pich, Cambodia

"The work I did was to carry the stones and mud in the construction work on my back for 6 hours every day."
— Sonam Kabo, Nepal

"Women have experienced low self esteem and respect in the church so far. This is very sorry when we view that they actually have participated in the church movement since the beginning of Christianity."
— Lee, Seong Heon, Korea

97

"Last Monday was traditional Chung Yan Festival. In that day we used to go to the grave of our family to memorize them ... worship dead spirit will bring good luck to the living ... after I and my husband become Christian, we are more and less fall in trouble ... If we participate such festival which more or less carring ceremony of idol worship. I still trying to find a way which Jesus will agree with."   — Man, Suk Yee, NT, People's Republic of China.

* * * * *

I've been thinking about culture shock lately, as I have students coming over in January to this archipelago of 235 rocks and islands upon a squat mountainous peninsula with some borrowed new land, and want to tell them what to expect. Here are a few ideas about the progressive steps we move through:

1. There is a sense of excitement and almost giddiness at the spectacle of this Hong Kong. And many aspects are familiar and thus reassuring.
    This is fun!
2. There is a sort of bewilderment and tenseness that sets in as you realize how far from home and your culture you really are.
    This is scary!
3. Our way and our own ethnic identity is challenged and we feel anger toward the Chinese and complain.
    I really don't like this!
4. We begin to relax (hopefully) into the way it is here even though it is very different. We develop tolerance and greater objectivity and ways of coping.
    I can do this!
5. There is a new richness to our lives as we become a second person and celebrate a new way of being and relating.
    Let's do it your way!

* * * * *

I preach this Sunday at Tau Fong Shan's Pilgrim's Mass. On Monday I will preach in the seminary chapel demonstrating the use of saints' days. (St. Nicholas, Dec. 6th.) We will use the WOV (*With One Voice*) liturgy for the first time also.

12/12/1999

I went into mainland this weekend to try to contact Christians in a community where the government had taken away the buildings etc., of a parish started 107 years ago by the Basel mission. They have regained the old, run-down sanctuary but not the rest of the campus. They had hoped that a professor from LTS could come and preach once a month; but the government said that could not be permitted. I did have the privilege of giving a "greeting" which was based on the scripture and lasted 25 minutes. At least 500 gathered to hear the greeting (and not a sermon)! They sat outside, filled the dilapidated sanctuary, peered in the dirty windows and stood too far away to hear me, but, wanted to be close to their church again. As part of the fellowship we had bread and wine after reading First Corinthians 11. At another location, I then met with at least another 100 high school age youth. They are so hungry for anything they can learn about being a disciple of Jesus. God willing, I will return there. They have registered to be a three-self church and will get government approval for worship. They will not get the rest of their buildings back. (This paragraph is vague to protect those whose efforts are heroic in the faith. I'll write more on this when I am back in the states.)

I took my four Myanmar students down to Causeway Bay for dinner. Deonal came along, too. We had genuine Burmese and Rangoon food. Lots of spice and fried eel, beer, curry, and laughter. With tears in his eyes, "Mr. Burma" said, "I have gone home for a little while tonight and I am comforted." "St." Pau told him he was always comforted when someone bought him free food!

I return home to California on the 14th of this month and will return to this Mountain of the Logos Wind on the 14th of January.

99

Report # 12: PLTS Students Experience Asian Culture
01/21/2000

It was a good month for me in the U.S. over the Christmas holidays. Our kids and grandkids gathered in Gold Canyon, Arizona. We played golf, hiked, rode horses in the desert, and ate some very good food. The week after they all returned to their homes we entertained thirty of my seminary classmates and spouses in our home for a three-day reunion (at our age it takes longer to celebrate and do almost everything). There was hugging, laughing, and tears of pain. We graduated forty years ago from the Hamma Divinity School of Wittenberg University in Springfield, Ohio. Most were now retired, some were just tired, several had died, and still others had hilarious stories to tell about their long ministries. At the foot of Superstition Mountain we communed together using wine from the Pfalz and lebkuchen classmate Willy Polster brought from Nürnberg.

I flew back to Hong Kong on January 12 to begin my second semester of teaching up here on Tau Fong Shan mountain in the Lutheran Theological Seminary. Two of my students (Henry from Myanmar and Sinaga from Indonesia) had gotten up very early, taken busses, and were there to meet my plane. When we arrived at my room in the dorm, the students had placed flowers and balloons all around. A sign in English hung from the ceiling, "Wellcome our Professor." The children, two Nepalis, a Korean, and Hephzi from India, came running with shouts of joy, "Uncle Jerry is back!"

That evening the students held a barbecue in my honor in back of the dorm. They paid for it with their own meager monthly allowance. Later that same day six of our PLTS students arrived for their two week's cross-culture experience so they were a part of the celebration also. We tried to recreate our "global dancing" of a couple months ago but somehow it was not quite the same. But this time some who had watched at a safe distance before joined in and even Chinese tried to do American boogie woogie.

I had paired by e-mail these PLTS students with Chinese ones here before coming over and they have really benefited from that already established relationship. Today we went to an ancient walled village named Kat Hing Wai, tomorrow to the big Buddha on Lantau Island. They will go out to various churches on Sunday. Some will go to Yuen Long with me where I will preach and catechize the Nepalis again. Our PLTS students have lectures in the mornings and travel most afternoons. Monday they will go into mainland by railroad accompanied by missionary and PLTS alumnus Steve Ray and DGM executive Dan Olson. In the evenings we hold reflection time when they gather in my now heated room to share journal entries and perceptions. I delight in their presence and sensitivities. Last Sunday they spent the day with missionary Valerie Peterson and observed her work with the Filipinas. They are awed by the stories of hardships and persecution which abound in our humble students from mainland, Myanmar, Cambodia, Nepal, and Indonesia.

On that first Sunday back I preached in the Kowloon Christian church because Lam Chiu Fai is a member there. This is what is called a "flat church." (Flat as way up in a high-rise apartment house; not flat as to evangelical zeal!) There are very few individual congregational buildings or homes either. Land is too precious for that luxury. There was a large gold cross against the front wall. On one side it said in Chinese "try to evangelize." On the other, "working together to serve." I was told to preach for at least 35 minutes there by the large baptismal tank. My translator was an architect. The liturgy consisted of reading scripture, singing hymns, and praying. There was no offering, but there was a box by the one door. When I arrived, the congregation was in small adult prayer groups. During the time after my preaching, the congregation paired up in twos and prayed for each other out loud. It startled me when the man next to me asked what he might pray for me. I then prayed for him after he answered the same question. While we all sang the Jewish tune, "Shalom, my friend," everyone got up and extended the peace. The worship was conducted by the lay deacons with the LTS graduate pastor only making a few announcements. The president of the deacons who presided wore a sharp business suit and tie on which was a large figure of Donald Duck.

At lunch today they announced my 66th birthday and 41st anniversary of ordination after which we had a cake and oranges to eat. My colleagues then gathered for cake and coffee. It has been such a God blessed life, marriage, and ministry.

I have begun my second semester classes: 43 students are enrolled in Church Administration which is offered in Chinese and English, ten each in Teaching the Catechism, and Preaching at Occasional Services. As of today I also have six tutorials and am advisor for three Master's theses. My new student from Germany, Katja Englehart, who has studied at Hamburg, will be a part of my breakfast table talks. I call her "Katherine the Great." She went with us to Lantau Island to see the Buddhist Monastery and the largest Buddha in the world on Saturday.

01/24/2000

Sunday (the 23rd) I took four of my American students to Yuen Long where I preach and catechize a Nepali group. It is rather pentecostal and startled my students. There are so many Nepalese here because under British rule they were the Gorkhas who did security work. Now they are mainly construction workers. It takes a day to go to Yuen Long and return. When we got back to Tau Fong Shan, the seminary president and family were waiting to take me for a typical celebration meal of pigeon and crawfish. We also had "pok" (pork) on a cabbage leaf. Upon my return, I had just started the reflection time for the PLTS students when all the dorm students called me to the common room for a surprise birthday party! Many had brought little gifts and they had a cake and candles. Sinaga from Sumatra, dressed in clothing I had brought him, read a poem about me he had so tenderly written which had all in tears. Two students who could not get there called on the phone and sang in Chinese. Then they led me to a table to read a message that was spelled out in candles: "WE LOVE YOU." Now I was in tears. It was very late when they let this 66-year-old leave to go to bed. Then came a happy birthday phone call from Pastor Irmgard Moser in Schmalenberg, Germany, at 4:15 a.m. Today, many of the students brought little wrapped gifts to class and presented them to me with both hands and a deep formal bow. Now a whole bunch of e-mails of congratulations. What a birthday and anniversary of ordination! I find it all very embarrassing but nice to be loved.

It is miserably cold! The temperature today is about 10c (50° F) but with a 75% humidity. There is no heat in the classrooms and for some strange reason the Chinese solution is to open all doors and windows so the damp, cold wind can blow through. When I ask why they say that it is healthy.

One of my biggest responsibilities this year is to prepare four students who will form new faculty in Myanmar (Burma). All the schools have been closed there for nearly three years. The military believes that education causes unrest. It is a hard ethical question for this school as to whether they should falsify documents in order for them to study at LTS (harder for the school than for me). Each must pay a 10% tax back to their government on all their income to do "research" here.

Sompong Hanpradit, Bishop of the ELC of Thailand, and Ishmael Herbrom, Bishop of Bangladesh, are both graduates of this seminary. Woo, Tin Fai, Bishop of the Malaysia Basel Christian Church, and Lee, Chee Kong, President of the Rhenish Church, are also alumni, as well as Smack Sothy who is General Secretary of the Cambodian Church Council. In this most ecumenical and international Lutheran seminary in the world there are eighty denominations and nineteen countries represented. God works mightily here!

These will preach

This morning the saintly old Andrew Hsiao, many years president of LTS and author of the new book, *The Lutheran Church in Hong Kong*, told of his first return in 1979 to the little mainland town where he grew up. Just before China began to open up and after thirty years' absence he returned and secretly took private communion to the ninety-year-old widow of the former pastor. She had no Bible, hymnal, or chance to worship all these years; but long ago she had memorized the psalms and could still recite them. And like many Chinese Christians she could pray. She insisted on receiving the sacrament on her knees. As he was giving her the bread, they heard someone coming up the stairs. Terror struck their hearts for fear they had been discovered. Then a seventy-year-old woman appeared who wanted communion also. It was the little girl Andrew's father had baptized sixty years before! Andrew said the widow prayed a prayer of thanksgiving like he has never heard before or after. They cried tears of joy and real presence.

Missionary Ted Zimmermann tells me that during the cultural revolution the secret Christians would gather close to the building which used to be their church and which now had been turned into a stable. They did this to acknowledge they were still Christians and worshipping in their heart.

Stella, whom I am advising on her Master's thesis, says the word "steward" in Myanmar is now used for people who are responsible for the safety of the people of a gathering of any kind. They serve as host, helpers of people in distress, and crowd control. They represent the event's institution. Consider our role as stewards of God's kingdom.

Report #13: Kong Hai Fat Choi (Happy New Year)
01/30 - 02/13/2000

At the request of president Lam, Tak Ho, I spoke yesterday to the board of trustees of LTS. All they have to date is a few church bureaucrats and a couple old men who meet once a year for dinner. We laid out for them what a working board might look like when they take seriously their role as stewards of this institution. Although I believe it was well received, I think I tried to do too much in one day. When they heard all a board could do, I heard a lot of "waaaaaaa" which might be translated into English, "wow!" It was a fault of my entire ministry to go too fast with my people. God forgives.

The Asian faculty also got very nervous when they got wind of the board taking responsibility for the school, as they have had a free hand in running the school till now. I have a hunch this will be the seventh milestone for this seminary founded in 1913 in Mainland, the previous six being (according to retired President Andrew Hsiao): 1) from isolation to cooperation; 2) from mainland to Hong Kong in 1948; 3) from mission to church, 1963; 4) from western to Chinese, 1971; 5) from Evangelical Lutheran Church of HK to a Union Seminary, 1977; and 6) from Shatin village to Tau Fong Shan, 1992; 7) *? and from faculty governed to board governed, 2000.*

News from home and racism here

These have been upsetting days for our international students. Sinaga is very concerned about Indonesia going to pieces and the terrible bloodshed between Christians and the predominate Muslims. Stella Min, a Karen tribe member from Myanmar, went into real grief for her tribe who are being chased out into Thailand where their desperation for medical help led to twelve of them systematically executed. Her tribe has been leading the revolt against the military regime for years. She may have to do her teaching in exile when she tries to return.

Twice recently we have experienced racism which deeply troubled me who tries to take seriously my role of spiritual father in which they have cast me. Two days ago two of my Burmese students were walking down the mountain when two Chinese ran after them and treated them like the illegals they are always searching for on this hill. (They come up here with a blue truck with a large yellow cage on it. They club and kick illegals and then throw them into the cage.) They were brutal with Henry and St. Pau even after they showed the LTS identification card. It is only by God's grace we did not have a real fight! Also when Deonal and the PLTS students and myself were going through the underground gates, an MTR policeman picked him out of the white and Asian hoards of people to check his card. He showed his HK resident card and his LTS card but was told he could not use a student pass because he is from Sumatra. I insisted he was a full time student with me but it was to no avail. The policeman was blatantly wrong, but could not lose face. Deonal bought a full fare pass in his usual humble manner.

The Asian secretary of the Mission Werks in Neuendettelsau, Germany, where I taught last year, made a visit. He was on his way to Papua New Guinea to visit their missionaries there. It was a favorite place of mission for Wilhelm Löehe, the father of the Mission Werks. We had such a great time talking in German and comparing notes on all my friends there. He was so interested in what I have been able to discover about Löehe's preaching which moved thousands to mission and I was so happy to find someone interested! It is another example of how this "School of the Prophets" is a literal crossroads of the Christian world wide family.

Chinese New Year's worship

We had a wonderful Communion service on Friday (the custom is once a month communion). A Swedish TV station filmed it all featuring our two Swedish missionary faculty members. It began outside the chapel with a dancing lion and the telling of a story about the origin of sin. The inside was all decorated in a Chinese New Year's theme. There were lots of red and paper posters. All of the students wore their native costumes and came forward to give the new year's greeting in their own language. Of course, the service was in Cantonese. Judy from Korea did a liturgical dance in her beautiful yellow and red gown. At the right time we came forward wearing our native dress (all I could come up with was an American flag tie). We joined as one family celebrating the presence of Christ with us. God must have been so pleased.

We held a commitment camp this week for 33 youth from the Hong Kong churches. They stayed in our retreat center for three days and all of the faculty helped in the program. The emphasis was on vocation and the call. Many will no doubt be students here in the near future. I wonder if we do enough of this kind of confrontation and bold witness with our American youth?

The learning group I supervise was quite moved when Chim Pich from Cambodia, who was reporting on grief counseling, told how the Cambodians coped with the slaughter of so many by the now infamous Khmer Rouge led by despot Pol Pot. He said when their loved ones would disappear because of torture and assassination, they would take large bundles of grass, shape them into the likeness of the deceased by tying with country twine, and dress them like their missing loved ones. Then the friends would gather and grieve over the grass replica, stroking it and crying a loud wail. Once this was over they would dress the grass in black like the Khmer Rouge wore and punch, stab, shout, and shoot arrows at it screaming their anger. A calm would eventually come and they would depart in peace. Sounds like good grief therapy for us who hurt!

When I preached at Tau Fong Shan last Sunday night, Dan Olson brought his teachers, who had come out of China, to the service. The ELCA has six teachers of English in China right now. We are not permitted missionaries so this alternate strategy. They are paid by two sources: the ELCA provides $250 per month from a grant from Amity Foundation and the local school where they teach must come up with 1000 of their currency (worth about $150 U.S.).

Multicultural Learning

I have begun my second semester learning group which is made up of the students I offer tutorials and advise on their thesis writing. Here is the make-up of the group:

Dorottya Naggy from Hungary — Pastoral Care and Counseling in Prison

Deonal Sinaga from Sumatra — Pastoral Care and Counseling in the Parish

Suan Pau Thang from Myanmar — Evangelism and Church Growth and Relation between Pastoral Counseling and Psychology

Stella Min from Myanmar — Pastoral Care and Counseling Thesis — The Karen Tribe Family Structure and Implications for Christian Ed.

Chim Pich from Cambodia — Pastoral Care and Counseling

Rita Kabo from Nepal — the Nepali Christian Family

Peter Lam Chiu Fai from Hong Kong — Counseling the Homosexual

I will learn so much from their reports to the group and individual tutorials.

I must now prepare for the "year of the Dragon" and Chinese New Year vacation from February 4 to 14 when there are no meals provided. I will stock up on peanut butter and breakfast food and hope I can find milk which will last that long. Stella Min wants to cook rice for me, but I am not great on rice without anything on it. How insignificant these little struggles are compared to many of our sisters and brothers in the global family. It will be a quiet time when I can get back to writing on my *The Preacher's Workbook* for series A which has a deadline of next August.

I am so looking forward to a good friend's visit: former GTU President Glenn Bucher. PLTS professor Ted Peters had to cancel his meetings here. After having those six PLTS students here I now really miss them. They are great examples of real quality PLTS students preparing for ministry. The church will be well led by their spiritual leadership.

These will *not* preach

The folk wisdom tells Asian women that if they laugh without covering their mouths with their hand, "they will look like a monkey." This seems to inhibit laughter. We Americans seem rude to them with our boisterous laughter.

One Chinese colleague joked to me that New Year's was the only day the Chinese cleaned their houses! I guess Chinese traditionally clean their kitchens today so the kitchen god won't report them to heaven for a dirty kitchen. (Mabel Wu told me this seriously.)

Everywhere is the cell phone. I fear Chinese may soon evolve with a pressed-against-the-head left ear and a left arm frozen in the phone holding position. When I walked into the bathroom yesterday, I heard a loud voice talking in one of the stalls. Sure enough, it was a man sitting on the toilet talking on his cell phone! (I will resist any puns here although the possibilities for some of Luther's anal humor are almost overwhelming.)

Sunday on Tao Fong Shan

We have thick fog up here on Tao Fong Shan. The humidity is a heavy 95%, and we have had some "rain patches," as they call them. The temperature is a warm 22c. If it rains more, they will warn against "hill slips" (familiar San Francisco Bay area problem). The radio just announced that because of fog there had been two collisions in Hong Kong Bay which confirms my suspicions that they really don't have control of who goes where with all those ships, ferries, junks, and cargo ships. They said visibility was less than 200 meters. Sounds like the proverbial "Chinese fire drill"!

I spent my Sunday with a hot water shower, corn flakes, and climbed the 121 steps to my office where I prepared my sermon for next Tuesday's chapel and then wrote a chapter for my book. I was the only one up there where everything is wringing wet. All the windows steamed over and all the floors are sweating and very wet. This is damp! Tonight I will go to worship at Tao Fong Shan Christian Center in the newly remodeled Buddhist-looking building. I am glad to be back worshipping in that unique space.

Last evening was something else! Because it was Valentine's Day for the Chinese, my students (two Cambodian, one Indian, one Hungarian, and one German) and I took the railroad toward the border town of Lo Wu to visit two of our Chinese students in their flats. This is a very rare event when they invite a person into their home. Almost all entertaining is out at restaurants.

First we went to Punkin's flat (so called because she helped me make a pumpkin face for Hallowed Eve). It was one room up on the fourteenth floor where all living is done. Locks and security were elaborate. She cooked everything in a wok over a propane heater. We had fresh crab, chicken wings, and shrimp. The Indian brought curried chicken. And there were mustard greens, too. They also had rice wine and brandy. She is the only Christian in her family and belongs to a Lutheran congregation in the nearby high rise.

Then we walked for one-half hour to a walled village where they were holding another New Year's celebration with lots of gun powder, fireworks, music, offerings to Buddha, and gambling. I found the fireworks frightening. Stuff was set off all around us without any organization. It must be like being under fire in combat. But there was so much smoke, it did sort of drown out the garbage and sewage stink present in walled villages where they live so close together. Mei Yee motioned for us to hold our nose as we walked to her little two-story two-room house where she lives with her brother. Because she is the only Christian, there were two little Buddhist altars and the usual fruit offerings in her house for which she apologized. She wanted me to tell her it was OK to have them there where she lived. I assured her they would do her no harm, Jesus would understand, and they are very important to her brother. Everyone then relaxed and we sat down to drink a dessert soup and eat some oranges.

It was very noisy there where people live on top of each other. It's no wonder they speak so loudly wherever they go! I did notice her bed had a mosquito net. The old separate kitchen was still there which was a shack with a brick fireplace for wood burning and a huge wok no longer used. There was an indoor toilet which by then I was glad for.

The two students then made a grand announcement to all the neighbors now assembled that this was the biggest day of their lives because their professor had come to their humble homes and honored them. It seemed to me I was the one being honored! We headed back to Tao Fong Shan where we had to enter very quietly as it was 12:30 a.m. and that is way past the curfew, unless one has special permission to be off campus for more than four hours.

02/21/2000

A bomb discovered

They found near Ya Mei Tei underground station at Jordan today an un-exploded World War II bomb. Some construction workers were digging a new foundation and came across it. They had to

111

evacuate thousands before disarming the fifty-year-old explosive that had lain there passively all this time. In boarding the KCR (train), I must have walked over it a number of times! I wonder what other potentially wounding instruments lie just below the surface I walk on? I also wonder how long the evil of the past lies ready to explode in our present? Still legible on the bomb was, "made in the U.S.A."

Jesus on the flip side (these will preach)
The pastor who serves the seminary as chaplain, Patrick Chan, told me today that during the cultural revolution in mainland it was against the law to honor anyone but Chairman Mao. You had to have a large picture of Mao hanging in your home. The Christians used a double frame with Mao on one side and one of Jesus on the other. In the villages like where he lived, they kept the Jesus side out most of the time. When the People's Liberation Army came to town, they all turned the chairman Mao side out. Once when a solider discovered the two sided pictures, he died of a sudden illness on his way to report them for their disloyalty (Pastor Chan said that the Buddhists did the same thing). More than once, as an adult, he has turned a picture over to see what is on the other side, only to find old yellowed wrapping paper.

02/27/2000

Stella's fear
Stella Min is from Myanmar (formerly Burma) and a member of the Karen tribe which recently took over a Thai hospital demanding medical help for their families. Twelve were slaughtered after surrendering and were pictured on the cover of *Newsweek*. She will return to her country to teach in a new school of theology there. Here she is taking a tutorial from me in Pastoral Counseling and I am her advisor in writing her thesis on the Karen tribe's family structure and opportunity for Christian Education.
During my class on Teaching the Catechism she became very quiet, almost panicky, and kept watching the window and door.

After class I asked what was wrong and she explained that as we were considering the first commandment and Luther's meaning to it she could not teach such a thing back home. Stella said the military had asked the Buddhist monks to go through the Bible and announce why it was all wrong. Since that time it has been very dangerous to make the claim that only our God is true God and that we should "... have no other gods." If she did so, it might mean her arrest and the closing of the seminary there (which does not use the word seminary).

It was the first time I have witnessed such fear of saying out loud that God is our God (except for the times as parish pastor I have asked Lutherans to witness to their faith!). She forgot for a time she was not under her home military government and looked as if they would come to get her at any moment. The words whispered at home but openly spoken by these students were so scary for her to hear. How for-granted we take our religious freedom.

I later held a learning group session in which Stella Min was in attendance. I learned more: She revealed that her brother-in-law was taken from their home one evening for speaking against the military and admitting he was a Christian. They didn't know where he was or if he were alive or dead for two years. Then he was found by her sister in a prison where he has been for seven years. No wonder she is afraid when people around her speak about "no god but our God"!

The Bataks' smoke

Many times I have told you of my Batak student here from Sumatra island, Indonesia. Yesterday I went with Deonal Sinaga to an Indonesian store in Tai Wai and in the back ate with the owner some Indonesian food I cannot name. It was quite good. All one bowl mixed together and then very hot spice mixed in. The napuran gave it a red color.

Sinaga is preparing to teach at STT-HKBP seminary in Pematang-Siantar where I taught a couple years ago. After consulting with my daughter Bethany on e-mail about it, he decided to admit to me he had started smoking while an intern in Sumatra and he has not been able to give it up altogether here. Because of my

Stella Min wearing Carol Schmalenberger's dress

lectures on the stewardship of one's health and our private conversations about the Bataks' use of cigarettes in church, he has been afraid to tell me.

He told me what I already knew about their culture: that smoking with others is a matter of courtesy and hospitality. If you are a male, you hand a cigarette to a person to say welcome and smoke with them to say you are their brother. If there is a conflict on the church council (and there are many), they all sit down and the pastor smokes with them while they discuss it. It serves this social function like a peace pipe did for Native Americans! Just after the benediction, all the men pull out their cigarettes and smoke in the pews while the older women chew their napuran and the sanctuary turns very blue with a smoke not of the Holy Spirit.

I think he will quit here where very few smoke. But I doubt it will be possible in Sumatra, as he would be considered "aloof since studying abroad" if he refrained there. (I have no answer for his struggle.)

Mrs. Kung is expecting

Henry Siang Kung's wife back in Myanmar (formerly Burma) is due to have their baby this month. It will be a four hour drive, in a rented car he will need pay for, to the nearest village where there is a doctor. She needs to have a C-section. That means he will also have to see that his brother takes along an electric generator and money to pay the doctor, the hospital, the nurse, and the cleaning person. He must also bring along whatever medicine will be needed. All is to be paid before any procedure will be started and the family will have to provide their own food for her as well. We have one nervous father here! There are two phone lines into the village and one can be used only by the military, so it may be a while before we know how it all goes.

These will preach

Andrew Hsiao, former President of LTS, told me of his mother in Hunan Province during the Cultural Revolution. As an old woman she was called into their Lutheran church building and put on trial for being a Christian, forced to renounce her faith in the sanctuary of her own church. She never recovered from it. I am not sure he has either.

A Burmese student told how an older Buddhist man in their tribe had glaucoma and needed eye surgery. All the Christians contributed all the money they had and took him to Rangoon. The surgery was successful. He asked to be baptized and now is one of their best evangelists. Rice Christian you say? I'm not so sure.

Yi, Narith from Cambodia wrote in a paper for me: "... we produced one to two hundred local congregations between 1989 to 1993. The congregations are still existing." He got a video of Jesus' life and went around Phnom Pen with a few fellow Christians. "We were all new converts — an occasional American Missionary from Campus Crusade for Christ visited the country. I used to pray, fasting once a week, and live a most simple life. Not many people want me to marry their daughters (he is still single). I had nothing, not even a proper dress and shoe, but relation with congregational members and joy in God."

We write best what we feel most. Ruth, one of our older students and a recent Chinese Christian, won an award for writing the best Christian tract. In accepting the award she told how she had opposed Christianity all of her life and now that she had become a Christian, she wrote the gospel tract hoping her husband would read it and believe. He was not there to see her receive the award.

This and that

Belching is acceptable and everywhere. The dining hall is a cacophony of low and higher pitch belches. TV ads for good hotels, restaurants, and kitchenware called Ikea end with a full belch. This is less startling to me than the spitting out of bones on the table while eating. Then there is the greasy rag used to wipe (smear) the table after the meal ...

During the sermon by an East Indian at Tau Fong Shan someone set off a whole bunch of fireworks. Maybe that's what we need do about our preaching. He was so stunned he lost his place and for a couple moments there was life and fun in the gospel. I laughed out loud and should not have done so. But God smiled.

It was announced on the local news tonight that 270 elderly Chinese commit suicide *each month* in Hong Kong.

Hiking across Tau Fong Shan with some of my international students after sitting through a pastor's dreadful theological reading (read sermon), I asked Thang Suan Pau what he thought of the sermon. He responded in his broken English: "No feeling." The rest of the group, who were afraid to criticize in my presence, roared. Pau grinned from ear to ear for he was understood ... and so right.

During a test today I discovered a woman in the back of the room talking on a cell phone. She may have had someone on the outside feeding her information from the book. While I had asked questions calling for them to contextualize the answers, the Chinese students gave memorized statements from the book. I think this reflects the type of education in their school system.

117

The Finns have a saying, "throwing water on a goose." It means "it won't sink in." They may be describing a kind of educational process as well.

Yesterday, March 17th, they found another World War II bomb unexploded. It was not far from here, close to Hong Kong University where they were excavating for some construction. The University and area around it were evacuated.

In my learning group one of the students told of being so desperate for food that he smuggled contraband across the border into China and was caught. He was placed in a jail cell ten feet by six feet with ten others for three days. No toilet. Had to sleep standing up. Finally they needed him to speak English for them so they demanded his family pay a fine and let him out eventually.

03/19/2000

The tension was very high here over the election in Taiwan and we had a special prayer session in chapel for peace. The Taiwanese students downstairs from me were very upset. It is now Sunday morning and the tension over the election has eased a great deal. I will spend the day writing on my book and then go to Tau Fong Shan Christian Center for worship tonight, as I do not preach anywhere today. But the congregation in Mainland where I gave the 22 minute greeting has asked me back!

In my lecture last Monday I demonstrated my homiletical theories by telling them how I would do this Sunday's sermon four different ways. Now ELCA missionary John LeMond says he really feels the pressure since he has to preach tonight. We have become good friends.

At the LTS annual lecture I gave last week, there were more than 400 in attendance. It was held at the Methodist Church close to Truth Lutheran in Kowloon. Many pastors and faculties were there, as well as students from several seminaries. Our students chartered two buses to transport them. The president of the Methodists and the president of the Lutherans of Hong Kong gave responses. Lam, Tak Ho was thrilled with the results, as it went very well.

Before the lectures, I taught my class of 43 here and then addressed a banquet of Doctor of Ministry students where they celebrated my willingness to return in March and April the next few years to work with them.

No word yet about Henry's wife. I took him and Deonal down to Shatin for dinner last night.

Language

In my class on preaching and doing the occasional services, a Korean student trying to do the marriage service asked the Cambodian groom to repeat the words after him, but was not clear. So the groom promised to be *unfaithful* to the bride until death parted them!

Eddie, translating from Chinese to English for us in chapel, put the English this way: "Jesus said, 'I am the life of bread.' " A petition in a recent prayer went: "Help us to respond heartlessly, O Lord." Howard, the translator, sensed it was wrong and changed it to: "Help us to respond heart-listlessly." You understand, Lord. It's the language.

Korean student Kim He Joo kept talking of "refreshment." I finally discovered she meant revival! It works.

A "prawn brain" in Burmese means someone not very smart.

Sonam Kabo tells me that "persecution means to give birth to a new church for Nepali Pastors."

International Performers

The little children of our married students decided they would put on a play for their parents and the other dorm residents. Our little Korean girl, "Amazing" Grace, came to my door with a torn piece of paper marked for "unkle Jerry." In our little courtyard they had placed six plastic chairs for reserved seating. One better chair was in the middle for me. The Indian girl told the Batak student he couldn't sit on any of them because he was in "standing room." Priya Kabo from Nepal seemed to be the stage manager. It then dawned on them that they had spent all afternoon arranging for seating and tickets but had not planned what the entertainment would be! So the all-girl cast of one Indian, one Korean, one Chinese, and two Nepalis would huddle on one side of the "stage" and then the other side, deciding what they could do. Most of the time the language among them seemed to be English; but not always understood. The Indian Orthodox Priest next to me roared with delight like I have never heard him. We witnessed singing in native tongue, cartwheels, improvised on the spot dancing, nursery tales I did not recognize, and a lot of pushing each other out on the stage to reluctantly do something in addition to giggling. The applause was spontaneous and often. It drew out of their rooms all the students who had not been a part of the select invitees. The performers announced the show was over, they had to get to bed, and the adults should clean up and put everything away. They made their exit stage left.

The worrisome news today is that a Guangzhou-based Christian pastor named Li Dexian has been arrested again for "illegal preaching." This is the town where I will be lecturing in a Guangdong seminary on May 18-20. This 48-year-old pastor has refused to register his church in Huadu for the last ten years and so has been locked up this time for fifteen days. Daniel Kwan writes that "Hundreds of villagers worship at his church each week despite the police harassment."

The South China Post reports (April 14, 2000), "100 Falun Gong members arrested in violent scuffles with police in Beijing April 13 after group members flocked to Tiananmen Square." The officers kicked and punched demonstrators who were mainly middle-aged women. The police also ran around the square confiscating film from tourists who had taken pictures of the melee. My Christian friends find the Falun Gong trouble, as a bad omen for any organized religion. The government lumps them all together.

These will preach

Siang Kung from Myanmar (Burma) writes: "During WWII my grandfather lost one of his eyes. He got treatment from a witch doctor. The witch doctor told my grandfather that one who is greater than the witch doctor is coming. On the next day, at his surprise, my grandfather met a Christian evangelist from whom he heard the name of Jesus for the first time. From that day my grandfather stopped going to see the witch doctor. When the war was over my grandfather become a Christian. He was the first convert in the region and was excommunicated from the village community. In the midst of many dangerous things, my grandfather preached Good News. Later the villagers believed in Jesus Christ and my grandfather became their pastor."

"Since 1966 the door of my country has been closed. No foreign missionary is allowed to come in and Christians are not allowed to go abroad. Though the church grew rapidly, theological education is left behind. Seminaries and Bible Schools founded by the missionaries are badly in need of teachers." Siang Kung was the Vice-Principal of Zomi Theological College where he taught twenty hours per week. He is now doing a Th.D. program in Christian Education at LTS after studying previously in England.

I preached in Chapel on the text of Jesus' words about the rich man and the camel through the eye of a needle. I have learned that in the Tiddim version of the Bible for Burmese, it is an elephant instead of a camel. That is contextualization.

One Sunday I preached at an old-time Union church in Kowloon where English is spoken. Several Bataks were there and I could greet them in their Batak language. Because it was communion Sunday, I had planned to preach on the "forgiveness meal." Then I spotted in the bulletin (which one of my students from India had typed) these words: "Now we will take the bread and win." Yes, we do win and it is a feast of victory. It was too good not to use and a new sermon came out on the spot!

Colleague Peter Lee drew for me the Chinese characters for peace: rice in mouth, which is the economic basis for peace; a roof over one good woman, which is the sociological basis for peace; and two hearts parallel, which is the spiritual basis for peace.

My "family" met for supper last night to meet Carol, who is here right now. Yi, Narith from Cambodia told Carol that when his country opened up to Christianity after Pol Pot, he was one of the first to be baptized. There were nearly 300 of them baptized in a river he claims runs one direction for a portion of the year and the other direction the other part of the year! (The student body is divided into families of about eight to ten with a mix of nationalities. One or two faculty belong to each family.)

Chinese April Fool's Day

Now they know April Fool's Day well here. Because I have suspected the Chinese would be helpless without their chop sticks, I went to the dining hall early and took all the chop sticks and the few knives and spoons and hid them. As the students who eat breakfast here arrived, I said I believed someone (perhaps the Baptists) had broken in and stolen all our utensils. They tried to fix the oats and toast in all kinds of ways. Then the two cleaning ladies arrived

122

and began to rave about it in Chinese. I brought out the stuff. The cleaning ladies chased me around the dining room shouting in Chinese and laughing. It was such fun. At the library, I told Stella that I could not keep her appointment today because my wife told me our dog had died and I must return to conduct the funeral. (She is taking my course right now on Occasional Services.) I told the librarian that I had dropped four books in the fish pond on the way to return them! She turned white as a sheet. Finally I put a sign on the office door telling everyone to wish the Director of Development (Cynthia) a "happy birthday" and don't mention the note. After that everyone knew it was "Dr. Jerry" and it was April Fool's Day. My kids will recognize the symptoms.

The former president of the Graduate Theological Union, my good friend, Glenn Bucher, was here last week for a visit. On our hike to the Temple of the 10,000 Buddhas to celebrate Ching Ming day when Chinese visit their ancestors, he told me of a delightful experience he had eating breakfast in the mainland. He had ordered four fried eggs but they brought him four hard boiled eggs. He complained and the server said they were out of fried!

If you are talking to someone and the host pours more tea, you need not interrupt the conversation. Just put your hand in a claw like position and tap your fingers on the table. They will know it means thank you. Many years ago when the emperor was incognito and his loyal subjects wanted to "kow tau" him without giving away his identity, they started using this now well-accepted gesture. By the way, the host will keep your little cup full. The only way to stop drinking is to leave it full.

The first Westerner to preach in Buji

Carol went with me Sunday into mainland China near Shenzhen. The Buji "Three-Self" registered church which opened in 1994 requested that I come and preach. (There are no denominations allowed for the Christians there.) Up until now the government has not allowed any Westerner to preach, only bring "a greeting" which I have done before. And the specific directions were that the sermon was to be at least one-half hour. So they got a sermon by a Westerner for the first time in many, many years. I was told afterward that the rules which forbid it had not changed, they were just less concerned with them now.

Outside Buji church, Shenzhen, China

One of my students, Peter Lam, a Chinese Indonesian who speaks Mandarin as well as English and Indonesian, did the translating. It was in their 108-year-old building, formerly a mission compound, which had been recovered from the government in 1994. That was full, the little courtyard outside was full, and two rooms not connected to the main building were full. In one of them was a closed circuit television of the service. My guess would be about 600 inside and out and of all ages. The electricity went off about ten minutes into the service, a common occurrence. The sermon was on the raising of Lazarus and may have caused what happened after the worship. The sick flocked to me for prayers of healing. They would tell Peter what was wrong and then I would lay on hands and pray. Headaches, broken bones, an unruly child, a marriage going apart, colds, heart palpations (which I did not cause), poor eyesight, and "female problems" were all given. I was very glad no one said that his brother had just died! (John 11:32-44). It was a very draining experience, yet very meaningful to me. While I waited to teach the 75 youth, they continued to line up for the prayers in the back of that room.

The husband of the evangelist had tried to prevent this by announcing to the congregation not to approach me after the service and then tried to have some deacons usher me up stairs; but I refused to go saying that I wanted to greet the people. While this embarrassed Carol, it really brought the sick to me. After perhaps thirty of these, I told my interpreter Peter to lay on his hands and pray. So like in the New Testament Peter healed the sick ... again. It was a new experience for him. But some insisted it had to be the "elder" white man. Carol got some interesting pictures.

Buji church — prayer for healing by Dr. Schmalenberger

Chinese Haircut (this will not preach)

One afternoon I hiked down the mountain to Tai Wai. The place several male students told me about for a 45 HK dollar haircut was closed. So I walked into an alleyway where I could see the green, red, and white symbol for a Chinese barber shop. I don't want to ask now at the seminary if I may have confused that symbol!

Anyway, I went upstairs two floors and opened the door to be met by two young women. I asked them, "How much for a haircut?"

125

in English. They sidled up against me and removed my ELCA cap as if to make an estimate. I asked again, "How much?" One pulled a 1000 HK bill from her partially covered bosom. I said "pang de" which means "make it cheaper" in Cantonese. About then I realized they were not pricing a haircut, I was not in a barber shop, and these were not Chinese barbers! There were no barber chairs but what looked like living quarters was to the side.

Now the problem was to get my hat back and make an honorable exit. The American had money and they were going to try to appropriate it. I couldn't think of any of my limited vocabulary except "good morning," "sit down," and "have a good meal."

Then I remembered what they taught me to say to the seminary dog which means "back off and don't bite!" It seemed to work. They backed off, I grabbed my hat off the table, and hurried down the steps. But they followed. I looked both directions, hoping to avoid being seen, and walked quickly down the alley. They were shouting after me what I think was a cheaper price, but I didn't hear it because I had removed my hearing aid for the haircut.

Three blocks away I got my hair cut by a real barber. I really didn't try to bargain at all. It cost ninety HK dollars. And on the way back here I kept watching behind me for those two "barbers"!

Etc.

In the Easter sunrise bulletin at Tau Fong Shan Christian Center we found out that the angel was Chinese who rolled away the stone for the women. It said: "Ho will roll the stone away from the entrance of the tomb?" (Mark 16:2b).

Carol returned to California on Tuesday, April 25. On the 26th of April I flew to Liberia, West Africa, to preach at the ordination of Lydia Manawu Weagba, the first woman to be ordained in the Lutheran Church of Liberia in its 140 year history. (Two graduates of Wittenberg's seminary started work there in 1860.) Twenty-two hours in the air each way via Paris, Ivory Coast, and then to Monrovia.

Report #17: Journey to Africa
05/09/2000

In 1987 Carol and I spent a sabbatical in the country of Liberia, West Africa. At that time we took a young Kpelle woman teaching in the Totota Lutheran School with only a high school education to her father and explained we wanted to send her to Teacher's College and then seminary to become the first woman pastor in the Lutheran Church of Liberia. John Manawu, her father, ordained in 1962 claimed, "It's not natural." Lydia finished the Teacher's College at Kakata and then began her theological training at Gbarnga School of Theology. The bloody civil war broke out and one of the war lords took over the seminary. We flew her out to Nigeria (not a wise choice of countries) where she had to start over. Problems developed there and she had to go to yet a third school of theology, graduating over a year ago. Now it was back to Liberia where there was an uneasy peace for a year's internship.

Then came the invitation from Bishop Sumoward Harris. Having been started 140 years ago by Wittenberg College, seminary graduates Morris Officer and Henry Heigerd, the Lutheran Church of Liberia would celebrate its 140th anniversary and ordain new

Ordination service (left to right): Bishop Sumoward Harris, Dr. Schmalenberger, The Reverend Lydia Manawu-Weagba, and The Reverend John J. Manawu

127

pastors April 27-30. They wanted me to keep my promise of twelve years ago to come and take part in the ordination of their first woman pastor.

The trip from Hong Kong was not easy. I flew to Paris, and then to Abidjan, Ivory Coast, and then into Monrovia arriving on Friday afternoon. The celebration (God Palaver) had already begun at Trinity Lutheran, Matadi, on the outskirts of Monrovia. A delegation led by Bishop Donald Main of the Upper Susquehanna ELCA companion synod was already there. They have done marvelous things for the Lutherans of Liberia. Like none other I know, with the leadership of Robert Bradford, these Lutherans know how to be a companion synod!

I stayed at the twice nearly destroyed guest house in the walled Lutheran headquarters. The city is a burned-out, war-destroyed collection of buildings now occupied by squatters. Since the war ended in '95 there have been no water, electricity, sewer, dependable telephone, mail, or employment. Few schools are open and garbage rots in piles in the streets. Lutheran World Federation/

Three leaders of the Lutheran Church of Liberia, all graduates of PLTS, Berkeley, California (left to right): Reverend Tokpa Songu, Bishop Sumoward Harris, and Reverend Joseph Kpanie

World Service feeds many out of the compound. The war has set the country back many years and the people have now elected Charles Taylor, the one who started it, as their President fearing he would continue the fight until he was in power. An old alum of PLTS, Wilton Sankawulu, serves as one of his advisors.

With hand-held two-way radios for security (or a sign of authority) our Church leaders move about the ruined city. "Spoiled plenty" cars and trucks litter the yards of the compound. The Bishop sleeps 22 in his house. Our ELCA missionary nurse, Deanna Isaacson, came in from up country seriously ill and was evacuated to the U.S. Our three more recent PLTS alumni are Sumoward Harris, Joseph Kpanie, and Tokpa Songu. They are the Bishop, the General Secretary of the LCL, and a teacher at the started-again Gbarnga School of Theology. Another alum present, Benyam Kassahun, serves the DGM as Program Director for that area. We were all together in the Bishop's home on Monday.

On Sunday the elders, evangelists, and we clergy gathered dressed in our vestments at a crossroads and began a half-mile procession on a red dirt road led by a police band to the church. First came the Bishop doing a sort of dance step, then Bishop Main and

Procession for the ordination service

129

myself, next about thirty clergy of the church, then Elders and Evangelists. At one time there were probably 800 in the parade and the street was lined with curious spectators. My bald head began to burn so I borrowed a golf hat from Don Main.

The Matadi church is a tin roofed cement block structure which seats 800. Light bulbs strung down the center on a wire were powered by a generator which stopped working. A good PA system was run off a car battery. Outside was a cooler temporary structure of bamboo covered with palm leaves. A little farther away was a cook shack where women worked all day preparing a meal of rice, palm butter, chop, and potato greens. Out back was a place for two toilets but one was lying broken in the yard.

After the parade the service lasted from 10:30 a.m. to 3 p.m. Grebo, Kpelle, and Loma choirs sang songs about "Na Yala" (Kpelle for father God) and "Gaywolo-Gala" (Loma for sky God) with haunting rhythms. They often sang in a bent-over position slapping their thighs indicating songs for working. In an honoring ceremony Main, his wife Carol, and I were all presented beautiful native garments. I was called by the head of the LCL women, "our son of Liberia."

I preached on the symbols of ordination such as the stole, the laying on of hands, and called for all to be in a ministry of stewardship, witness, and servanthood, closing with a plea to treat well and celebrate their ordained women. "Ol'Man" said it was not American but African preaching!

Two men were set apart and then it was our Lydia Manawu-Weagba's turn. She wore my blue clerical shirt and collar which was much too big for her. But above that too-big collar was a radiance worth the trip to see and remember. After the laying on of hands I removed my stole and placed it on her. There were audible gasps and then that squeal of delight the Kpelle use when they are surprised. She was the sixtieth Liberian ordained in their 140 year history. A second woman, Dorothy Schellart, and two more men were then set apart also. Communion came next. It was blistering hot under that tin roof at this time of day. The Bishop read the assignments of the six to their parishes. I noticed one went to Degei for an *annual* salary of $2 American! That is a village I know well where the whole village has been burned down and now people are trying to return. He will have to grow his own food and build something in which to live.

Lydia has been assigned to the Matadi Parish as Associate Pastor and also acting Senior Pastor. She now lives in one room (which has a chair, small table, and two double bunk beds) with her new husband at the compound. He is a Methodist Pastor with his Master's degree and will teach at Gbarnga in Monrovia. He will have to do that without any books at all!

After the service was over the crowd surged forward to hug and congratulate Lydia. I feared for her safety as they all tried to embrace her at the same time and do their clicking hand shake. Then her father, John Manawu, an old war horse and saint of the church, kissed her on the cheek and with tears of joy streaming down his black deeply wrinkled face said softly to us both, "It's natural."

These will preach

Many years ago when the missionaries would start a school they would have to pay money to the parents of mostly girls to let

Dr. Schmalenberger with his young Liberian friends at Matadi, Liberia

them go to school. It was because the girls were good help at home doing cooking, caring for babies, etc. The money paid was called a "redemption."

A couple of the young people we sponsor walked me through the "war market." For a good half-mile on both sides of the street are for sale the things looted from homes and institutions during the war. They told me you can sometimes find stuff taken out of your own home that you must buy back again.

When the many offerings are taken, the Liberians often dance their way forward to drum and sassa music and then place what they have in a basket. How about that for a joyful giver whom God loves?

About The Lutheran Church of Liberia

Begun in 1860 by two men from Wittenberg College in Springfield, Ohio, with twenty girls and twenty boys freed off a slave ship, Morris Officer and Henry Heigerd are considered the founders of the church. It was called Muhlenberg Mission. Restarted and given solid foundation by their long tenure were Rev. David and Mrs. Emma Day from Susquehanna University at Selinsgrove, PA. (so the two Americans at this 140th anniversary were from Wittenberg and Susquehanna). For years this was the "white persons' graveyard" because of the many missionaries who died here. Many, many Wittenberg and Hamma people served in Liberia.

Present statistics:

Membership	63,548
Congregations/Preaching points	493
Evangelists	428
Ordained Deacons and Licensed Evangelists	45
Active Pastors	30
Pastors presently missing in action	2
Schools	81
Hospitals	2

A new book written by the late former President Roland Payne on the history of the Lutheran Church in Liberia is titled *A Miracle of God's Grace*. Payne died "of fright" being chased through the swamp during the recent war. Former missionary Joyce Bowers was responsible for putting the manuscript in its final form. She and her husband Louis were teachers there and her father-in-law, Rev. Louis Bowers, Sr., is still recalled fondly by the older Liberians for his ministry among them. The book is available for $15 (including postage) from Joyce Bowers: 926B Boxwood Dr., Mt. Prospect, IL 60056; vwordsmith@msn.com

The Seminary at Guangzhou

Two of our D-Min students, John, Dong-long Yang, Dean of
Guangdong Theological Seminary and another, the second vice
president, invited me to come to China to be the first Westerner to
lecture in this China Christian Council owned Three-Self school
of sixty students and six faculty. I accepted, getting there by a very
interesting one-hour ride on a Chinese train from the border at Lo
Wu (the regular Hong Kong metro transit trains do not cross the
border). We sped through dark green rice paddies and thick blue-
gray smoke of the shore-side unregulated factories of Guangdong
province. It was a Thursday and once there I got a too-short bed in
the nearby Victory Hotel!

The seminary is located in the former Anglican parsonage given
back to the church in 1986 on an island in Guangzhou (formerly
Canton) where the French and English once built their grand old
embassies and homes. The American consulate is close by. Sixty
students live dormitory style: boys in one large room and girls in

Guangdong Theological Seminary, Guangzhou, China

another, with their double bunks covered with mosquito netting. This arrangement often serves as their study room as well. Blue and red plastic buckets are outside the door, each one belonging to a student for bathing and washing clothing (which hangs everywhere).

Next door is the former Methodist headquarters, recently occupied by squatters, which the government converted into a factory, ran down, partially burned, and now turned back to the China Christian Council.

The "library" consists of some cabinets on the upstairs porch. Classes are held in two cluttered rooms which also serve for some as study areas. Many bicycles are parked in the space between the Seminary and the church. The six faculty have their personal desks all in one room. An outside "squat style" toilet is for all. Several employees are housed in shacks around the perimeter.

The plan had been for me to lecture to the entire student body and faculty and local Three-Self pastors on Friday morning. However the government would not grant permission to do so. But they said I could provide the regular Seminary morning devotions.

Faculty at Guangdong, Guangzhou, China

135

So we sang a hymn and then I gave a two-hour meditation on Discipleship! The Dean interpreted this into Mandarin. My scheduled lecture to the faculty also did not gain approval so we had a "tea" in another room where we were not observed and I made informal comments (which were approved) for one and one-half hours on "theological education around the world." The 84-year-old principal, Huang Guang Yao, attended. (Most of the pastors of the nine Christian churches and six preaching points of Guangzhou, with a population of six million, are very old men having been educated before the Cultural Revolution and surviving it.)

After lunch with the students in a crowded room, where each one furnishes her/his own tin bowl, and cook together, I went with the Dean to conduct a funeral.

Friday evening I spent with students who prepared my food and had many questions. A faculty person stayed nearby to help translate.

On Saturday morning John took me sight-seeing to a Taoist Temple and a Buddhist Temple and the large government assembly hall. We ate delicious Hakka food for lunch. While he did marriage counseling, I met privately with students in an off-campus room they led me to. We really struggled to communicate! They were absolutely convinced the Americans purposely bombed the Chinese Embassy in Kosovo. But they wanted to talk about freedom in Christ, about fundamentalism, biblical literalism, and about the church and politics. This was a select group of students who trusted each other and questioned the Three-Self patriotic movement and church and who knew well the secret "house church" movement. They had just returned from a compulsory week in Beijing where they were told by the government what they are to do as loyal Chinese pastors. We will try to keep contact with each other and I will pray for them and their struggle as to a Christian's loyalty to church and state.

Sunday morning I was not allowed to preach at the packed-to-capacity church, but they did say I could answer questions during a Bible study. So in that Colonial style former Anglican church, Rev. John, Dong-long Yang read Acts 2 and then asked that I answer the question, "What does this chapter mean?" And it was the same text I had prepared to preach on! So I took thirty minutes for my answer.

In my "Bible study" I told about my baptizing gospel singer Carrie McDowell and how she sang "O, Happy Day." As soon as I finished, a South African woman visiting that day came forward and began to line out "O, Happy Day," a young man stepped up to the piano and really swung that song, and a second South African woman took the translator's mike and joined the first. She sounded like Mahalia Jackson. Now the whole 600 mostly young people were singing and rocking in the pews. It was a joyous experience which brings goose bumps when I describe it still. The two Africans came over, hugged me, and disappeared.

I returned to Tau Fong Shan another way for a different experience. It was a three-hour bus ride to the border and then to this seminary where we are so fortunate to be well supported and housed.

A Mainland Chinese Funeral

This was "funerals wholesale"! The Government provides one funeral house for all funerals. It has twelve tiny parlors and two large ones for the wealthy. There are at least six to eight funerals going on at the same time. In an open space mourners wait with the person who will conduct the very brief service. A loud speaker announces what funeral is about to begin. All crowd into the little cubicle where the body has just been wheeled in and the right flowers displayed. Amidst the announcements, confusion, loud crying, din and smoke of Buddhist, Christian, Taoist, Hindu and "nothing" faith services, the leader tried to be heard. In the middle of the service an employee opened the back door to see if he could have the deceased yet. When finished (or slightly before) a button on the wall is pressed and piped-in scratchy music blares a discordant tune. All watch the irreverent attendant nail on the wooden lid with bone-chilling thuds. You can hear that same hammering sound all over the complex. Now all exit quickly so as to not be hit by the casket being wheeled to one of the six to eight hearses lined up at the curb with motors running. When they pull out (without any family) another hearse backs into that place at the ready for the next body to be cremated. In the cubicle another casket is wheeled in and flowers are changed. Pastor Dong-long Yang looked at me in frustration and pensively asked, "And how do I do your grief counseling in a setting like this?" It all took ten minutes not counting the waiting for our turn. And now I know how out of context my class on Preaching the Occasional Services was. Forgive my arrogance, God.

A little about Taiwan

The island of Taiwan was brought under Chinese control only during the last dynasty in the late seventeenth century, the same as Tibet. When officials in Beijing speak of Taiwan and Tibet as always having been an inseparable part of China, these facts are ignored. The Taiwanese students here at LTS love this new President and the even more audacious Vice President.

My last two weeks up on the mountain of the Logos winds, Tau Fong Shan, were busy ones of completing the academic semester at the Lutheran Theological Seminary and celebrating farewells in many different ways.

To finish my experiment in teaching across cultures in Cantonese and English, I needed to have a translator read to me the 32 term papers written in Chinese so I could give them a grade. The eleven remaining in my church administration class were in English. Then there were three thesis-writing students I needed to finish up. And the six tutorials I gave this semester needed oral exams which works better when the student's primary language is not English. Another thesis writer from Myanmar will use e-mail to continue to work with me on the subject of "The family structure of the Karen tribe and effective ways of doing Christian Education." I will also offer a course over e-mail to a Chinese student on "Discipling in the Parish."

These weeks were also taken up with many meals and parties of farewell and thank you's. Over and over students came to my door to offer little tokens of appreciation. These items were of little financial worth; but they were presented in such a formal and loving manner. It was the same in the Bavaria's Augustana Hochschule and Sumatra's STT-HKBP seminary. Perhaps there is something for us Americans to learn: the graciousness of gift-giving and leave-taking.

On Sunday, May 28, I walked down the mountain to Shatin and the KCR (train), then transferred to the MTR (subway) to Shek Kep Mai where I walked through the oldest public housing in Hong Kong. These massive concrete old dirty high rises of tiny rooms with shared toilets and kitchens are infested with rats, whores, drugs, and crime. Nearby on a small hill is Hong Kong's largest Lutheran church and parochial school where we held the graduation ceremony.

The one-and-one-half hour service, all in Chinese, was with great decorum. A banner over the altar made by Man, Suk Ye (who

139

now preaches with strong legs) read: "The 23rd. Graduation Service awarding degrees and certificates." About 1,000 watched as we awarded three Bachelors of Religious Education; eight Bachelors of Theology; eighteen Masters of Divinity; two Masters of Religious Education; eleven Masters of Ministry; two Masters of Theology; and two diplomas in Library Science. Then 54 from our extension night school for lay people in Kowloon received their certificates en masse. At the end of the service all decorum was waived and Asian picture taking pandemonium took over with abandon!

Then came a lovely banquet with faculty, staff, and board to honor departing faculty. A tearful moment for many of us was when Mabel Wu prayed for Dr. Lydia Chung who has breast cancer and is returning to Canada for more treatment. The students had a late night party for yet another farewell for me with "German water" which was quite touching.

A few shared their immediate future: One clergy couple dear to me from India may begin work in Queens, NYC's St. Paul Lutheran under the ELCA's Division of Outreach to do outreach to Indian people. Another couple will return to Kathmandu and may take over the pastoral leadership of an independent Lutheran congregation. A Korean woman will go home to be a full-time evangelist. Another Korean will start further studies at the Lutheran School of Theology, Chicago. And a Korean woman turned down by PLTS will begin her advanced studies at Luther in St. Paul.

After blessing a student mission team departing for Sabah, Malaysia, Monday morning, President Lam and his wife said their good-bye as daughter Athena waved from their third floor apartment, a thesis advisee blew a kiss, and a crowd waved as we departed from Tau Fong Shan in our taxi loaded with two suitcases, a carry on, the Batak Deonal Sinaga from Sumatra and Henry (Kati's Pa) Siang Kung from Myanmar (Burma). We inhaled the Logos wind as it blew in the cab's windows. On Lantau Island's new airport, Chek Lap Kok, I boarded Singapore Airline's 747 for the twelve-hour flight thinking of the many ways I could have done the whole thing much better and the many opportunities left unanswered. To God be the glory anyway!

140

Rita Kabo (left) from Nepal and Nisa Han (right) from Korea

These will preach

- I didn't put this in report #17 about Africa, but I can't get it out of my mind as I only tried to help *after* it happened. It haunts me. In front of an Abidjan, Ivory Coast, hospice where I had to stay overnight, I saw a solider in a taxi he had commandeered pull over another taxi. He pulled the driver out of the taxi and beat him on one side of the head and then the other. The driver knelt in the street and begged for mercy as the solider continued to scream at him and pummel and kick him. Many watched but no one intervened. He then reached down and took from his shirt pocket all the driver's cash for the day, got in the other taxi and demanded to be driven away. The beaten and robbed driver remained on his knees bleeding in the street. I think he said in French he will probably be beaten again by the owner of the cab when he tells him he lost the day's fares. "... And who is my neighbor?" I could only hand him a dirty under shirt out of my bag to wipe off and stop some of the blood.

- Dorottya Naggy from Hungary took a tutorial from me in Prison Ministry. She visits a women's prison on an island in Hong Kong harbor. Last Monday, as she was returning from her time inside the walls with the English-speaking prisoners, the staff ferry began to fill with water and sink. They sped full throttle toward another island beach and made it before being swamped. I asked her if she was recalling how Jesus walked on water? She replied, "No, I remembered how Peter sank, and then I looked for a life preserver!"

- According to Mei Yee Pang, another Hong Kong student, the word for "leader" in Chinese means collar and arm. It means to link together all the parts of a shirt, the parts which protect the main parts of the body. Sounds like Paul's definition of the church as "the body of Christ."

- In Liberia, one of the pastors presiding at the ordination told a story about the disciple Peter. Jesus told his disciples to go out

142

and bring back a stone to him. Upon their return Jesus turned the stones into bread. But Peter had brought back just a pebble and thus got very little bread. A few days later when Jesus made the same request all brought back their stones; but Peter did not return as soon. Finally he came back rolling a huge bolder! Jesus said, "Peter on this rock I will build my church."

- Chim Pich of Cambodia and Stella Min of Myanmar (Burma) both tell of the same practice by Christians in their countries: When they go to cook their rice, they always take the first handful of grain and put it in a special container which is set aside to be brought to the church each Sunday. This rice is then used to feed the poor and for the victims of the annual flooding in their countries.

- In our chapel service we were asked to pray for a recent graduate of this seminary, Fong, Ching Ye, who had fallen and broken a leg. After the service the seminary chaplain explained to me that her congregation would suspect she is not spiritual enough or this would not have happened to her. How easy it is to let superstition take the place of faith.

- The Chinese term "difang guannian" means a "sense of place." They will say they are from Shanghai even though they have never been there. Not their father either, but their *grandfather* was born there and left at the age of 25 never to return! The Bataks have a similar idea with their village of origin, "Bona ni Pinasa." We too have our place — our church and our baptism.

- At a worship service all in Chinese with no interpreter, I really felt lost. Then they began to sing "Holy, Holy, Holy." I joined in with gusto the hymn I have sung since childhood. Myself in English and everyone else in Chinese. I couldn't remember the third verse so I improvised: "Holy, Holy, Holy, I am glad to be here today. Early in the morning I would like to sing Chinese to thee, But I don't know the right words to say. If only I had learned Chinese I could sing praises like the rest of these. Amun." The young lad next to me grinned as if he were taking English in school.

And now I return to the U.S. and our comfortable home. You who have faithfully read all these long reports have served as my companions in what could have been a much more lonely year. Thanks.

From Pittsburg, California

Report #20
June 19, 2000

I had not expected to send out any more reports but thought you might find interesting e-mails from my students who studied with me up on Tau Fong Shan. They speak for themselves. Remember English is their second and newer language. She is (Karen) Tai Lin Chun, whom I call "Punkin" because she helped me to make a pumpkin face last October. After offering a course on Evangelism, I commissioned a group to go to the interior of Malaysia back with a primitive people to try out their new witnessing skills. She tells of her experiences. As you can tell she will take a course over the Internet with me this summer.

He is "Four Toast Henry" from Myanmar (Burma) who was given some cash to help with the birth of his baby daughter whom I named Katie. These are beautiful, new, and younger Christians and it isn't often we get to experience this kind of dialogue in the U.S.A. I assumed you would be interested.

* * * * *

Dear Dr. Jerry Schmalenberger:

How are you? I am now staying in Malaysia after the short mission trip. I will stay here for my field works until end of July. I may start another short mission in China if God supply my expanses. Otherwise I will take a intensive course in HK on Justification on Faith.

The short mission is very adventurous and we really experience a lot from it. First of all we see the great things that our Lord has done in the universe. He creates all creatures with his wonderful amazing grace. Though we are of different people come from different places, we meet in a dimension of place and time and start our fellowship. How wonderful it is our body gestures greet each other without obstacle. We have a Sunday school teaching

145

Tai Lin Chun (Karen "Punkin") at Lutheran Church
in Yuen Long where she does her practical work

them to make a wordless chain and to twist balloon. We have arranged two special night activities with them. Since the adults are celebrating the Harvest season, most of them are drinking. They suck wine from a large pot until drunk.

There are many children because the women's only job is to bore baby. They have no birth control. The men go hunting and fishing. They rarely grow corps or cultivate land though they celebrate the Harvest season. They do not make any business. We may think that they are too lazy and their life is too simple. However they enjoy the way of life God gives them. They very satisfy and always bear smile on their faces. You will see children wondering around and they look very dirty but full of laughter. The children are very decent and obedient. We may think they are lacking of many and need helps and supply. However we never see greedy eyes staring at us. Their big and dark eyes telling you that they are content with who they are and what they are. Their beautiful voices reach Heaven like angels and telling us that life is simple and beautiful. We pursuit for infinite desire and never feel with satisfaction. We always fall in a lost when we are filled with all useless scientific products. Our minds are preoccupied with a lot of stuff and we always forget our God.

We try to bring something to them and we confront a contradiction. Shall we destroy their harmony life of simplicity? In my point of view it may be better if we help them to strengthen their knowledge of education. They can learn God deeply and put God's word in top priority and become more Christ-like. Also they may get rid of the bad habit of drinking. They may also learn to minister their churches and become autonomy.

I have started my internship in a church in Sabah. It is a Lutheran church of the Basel Christian Church of Malaysia. (BCCM) I will stay here for one and half months. My pastors are a pair of very nice couple. They are willingly to teach me about their experience of ministering church. There are about one thousand congregations. I am being monitoring by them and they will let me learn more about how a Lutheran Church integrates with cell development. They also have Children and Youth ministry.

During this period of time I have to prepare three sermons. The first sermon must be finished on 2nd of July and the other two have to be handed on mid and end of July. The first one is Mark 5:21-43, a dead girl and a sick woman. I need not preach on the pulpit. They want to teach me in writing and train me to be a speaker of God. They hope that I am brave enough to preach and to evangelize too. It is not an easy task, may God's Holy Spirit fills in me and empowers me to write what He wants me to write.

The final assignment is to finish the paper with you. I will probably choose the topic of "the ministry of discipling and how I will do it as a parish pastor." I have just finished reading your book of Preparation for Discipleship. Before I start reading the word "corporate" come into my mind. I just wonder whether you agree with corporate development for a church in discipleship training. I discover this word in part II: How disciples live out their faith. As a witness to faith we have a corporate story to tell, a story about being God's people in a particular community. Also you have described the church ministry is God's business for clergy. I think there may not be wrong if we treat our ministry like a corporate party similar to a company.

In reading your book, it reminds me many beliefs of Christian faith for the Lutheran church. There are ten words to describe church, sacrament of baptism and communion, the three creeds and the doctrine written on the book of Concord and Lutheran Catechism. I am shamed of my little knowing about them as a disciple of God. Lord has mercy on me and gives me wisdom to love them and understand them all. Please pray for me as I will pray with Dorottya on every Tuesday on one o'clock. I will remember you on my prayer too. I hope I may read those books first and discuss with you later about my writing. I will be much appreciate if you give me some hints in reading those books. What subject I should concentrate to or method in reading them.

Once again I would like to give thanks for your patience with me. I especially thank you for the time we share in Hong Kong and the knowledge I learnt from you. You are really a good shepherd and professor. You kindness make us feel comfort to be with you and share with you. I appreciate very much your generous hospitality to all students. You love is so great that you never look down on us though you are such a great scholar. I like to call you Father Jerry because you really like a father to us. Thank you for all and I hope to hear from you soon.

In Christ, Karen, Tai Lin Chun

*　*　*　*　*

Dear Father Jerry,

How nice it is to read your e-mail. Thank you again for the toaster and other helps.

My family, baby Katie and my wife Meng, and all are fine. One news is that on 5 June, my younger brother (who was arrested and put into the cell for days) and wife got the first baby (a boy). I sent them one hundred US dollar from the gift of your students through the Burmese student (Rev. Vungh Lian) from Chung Chi College. He has already left for Burma. The exchange rate is US $ 1 equal to Myanmar Kyats 350. You can imagine how happy they will be.

One of the news from US friends is that United Pentecostal Church in my town was closed by the authorities and the pastor also was in prison for the time being. I do not know the reason. They ask us to pray that the Church will be open again and the pastor will be released soon. Some times, it is very unfortunate that non-believers cannot understand Christian hymns and religious activities. For example "Onward Christian Soldiers" may be a very serious political one for them.

We can do nothing for you but our simple prayers to God. Even in prayers, many times, we do not know how to pray. But the Bible tells us that the Holy Spirit will interpret our prayers to God better than we do (Rom. 8:26).

With respect and love, Four toast Henry

Addendum — Hong Kong Alums Meet

It may have been the first every PLTS Hong Kong alumni association meeting which took place in March in the Fung Lum restaurant, Tai Wai, Hong Kong.

Retired President of PLTS and now a Global Mission Volunteer with the ELCA's Division of Global missions, Jerry Schmalenberger called the little group together in his favorite restaurant at the foot of Tau Fong Shan mountain where he is serving as Visiting Professor of Practical Theology. It was not their first such meal together in the New Territories — or in Berkeley.

Solomon Wai-Kwok Li is doing further study and teaching parochial school. His wife, Janny Wai-yee Ho, is serving as the assistant pastor at St. Paul, an Anglican church, in Hong Kong. They both were "hooded" by Dr. Schmalenberger when they graduated from PLTS in 1997. Their pre-school son, Jonathan Ming-chit Li, was well known to the Delaware Apartments residents.

Christian Church — Tau Fong Shan
in Shatin, New Territories, Hong Kong

The Li's live on Peng Chau, a beautiful outlying island, commuting by ferry daily to Hong Kong.

Also in attendance at this reunion of alums was Solomon Hon-fai Wong who was an exchange student at PLTS in 1996. After serving in the ministry in Hong Kong for a brief time, he returned this year to our sister seminary, also on a mountain top, the Lutheran Theological Seminary where Schmalenberger has been teaching. After receiving his first degree, Bachelor of Theology, he will now complete a Master of Divinity.

Solomon is now married to Ackie Chung-Kwan Cheung, a recent graduate of LTS, who is a pastor at Ward Memorial Methodist church in Kowloon. They also live in Kowloon in the New Territories. She is presently being supervised by Schmalenberger in group dynamics.

The little group of young adults, a little boy, and an old retired seminary president ate Chinese food, laughed, prayed, remembered their precious days at PLTS, talked of present struggles and joys, toasted their beloved American seminary, hugged, and departed. Others in the establishment wondered who these people were. And where have they been to develop such a deep bond of memories and friendship. Their audible cry of amazement was a waaaaaaa!

— Jerry Schmalenberger